4

297
M952-P   Pike, Edgar Royston.
              Mohammed; prophet of the religion
           of Islam. New York, Praeger, c1965.

J

              1.Muhammad, the prophet. I.Title.

                          M F - JAN 12 '70

Mohammed

PRAEGER PATHFINDER BIOGRAPHIES

ARISTOTLE:

Founder of Scientific Philosophy
by Benjamin Farrington

CHARLES DARWIN:

Pioneer in the Theory of Evolution
by H. E. L. Mellersh

Mohammed

PROPHET OF THE RELIGION OF ISLAM

E. ROYSTON PIKE

FREDERICK A. PRAEGER, *Publishers*

New York · Washington

BOOKS THAT MATTER

Published in the United States of America in 1969
by Frederick A. Praeger, Inc., Publishers
111 Fourth Avenue, New York, N.Y. 10003

Library of Congress Catalog Card Number: 68-55017

Printed in the United States of America

Contents

4

List of Illustrations

Mohammed

I

Early Days in Mecca

"*Allahu akbar!*" It's just getting light. Already there is a golden glow above the horizon in the east, where the sun's fingers are reaching up to pull away the dark curtains of night. Most of the world is still asleep. Nobody seems to be about. There's nothing to be heard, not a footstep, not a dog's bark or a cock's crow, nothing—save this strange high-pitched call coming from somewhere across the street.

"*Allahu akbar!*" There it comes again, and there, if you jump out of bed and look out of the window, you may see the man who is sounding it—a man in a long robe, with arms upraised, standing in a little open gallery near the top of a high, pencil-shaped tower. "*Allahu akbar!*" Again it comes, and yet again, four times in all. Then the voice goes on, and this, translated into English, is what the man is saying:

Allahu akbar! God is most great!
I believe that there is no god but God!
I believe that Mohammed is God's Apostle!
Come to prayer, come to prayer!
Come to salvation, come to salvation!
Prayer is better than sleep, prayer is better than sleep!
Allahu akbar! God is most great!
There is no god but God!

This is what we should have heard this morning if we had awakened in Algiers or Cairo, in Damascus or Baghdad, in Karachi or Djakarta. As the earth speeds through space in a new day's journey round the sun, the call to prayer sweeps along with it. And everywhere, the sleepers awake and, stumbling drowsily from their beds, stand, bend, then kneel and prostrate themselves in the time-honored ritual of adoration.

Over the roofs of famous cities the call rises and falls, and it echoes among the bee-hived huts of villages, which are far too small for their names to be found on even the largest-scale map. It summons the rich man in his palace and the peasant in his hovel. It rebounds from the Pyramids of Egypt, and sounds above the temple gongs of India. Chinese peasants in their blue coats and trousers have heard it, and so have the workers on the dawn shift of the collective farms of Soviet Asia. And, deep in the jungles of Central Africa, a man who only yesterday was a pagan, bowing down to gods of wood and stone, steps out into the sunlight and says his prayers in the new-fangled way that he has just been taught. Perhaps he throws just a glance at the blood-smeared idol that lies broken and dishonored in the gutter, but there's no fear in his glance, only contempt. For he is a Muslim now, and Muslims don't worship gods made with men's hands. Henceforth his god is Allah, the

Great, the Compassionate, the Merciful: *"Allahu akbar!"* And
the second article of his simple creed is, "I believe in Mohammed, who is the Apostle of Allah!"

Mohammed . . .

Our story begins in Arabia, the great slab of land that lies
where Africa and Asia meet. It is an ocean of sand, where,
until the coming of the truck, the best means of transporta-
tion was the camel. There are over a million square miles of
it, and it is 1,800 miles from one end to the other. It is a harsh
land for the most part, inhospitable and silent, with grim
mountains and burning expanses of red sand. Rivers run dry
most of the year, but where there is water there is greenness;
palms and fruit trees, dates and spice plants flourish.

Towns are few and far between. For the most part the
inhabitants are Bedouin tribesmen, living in tents of hair and
woolen cloth, and wandering about the desert from oasis to
oasis, waterhole to waterhole, with their camels and horses,
flocks of sheep, and herds of skinny goats. Yes, on the whole
it is a harsh country—one in which the ground is hard and
unyielding and from a brazen sky a fierce sun blazes down.

The Arabs are Semites, and belong to the great branch of
mankind that includes the Jews and at one time also included
the Babylonians, Assyrians, and many other famous civiliza-
tions. We do not know where they came from in the beginning, and hundreds of generations have left hardly a trace.
They have remained unknown as their land has remained
unknown. Even today there are vast tracts of Arabia that
have never been traveled by a human foot, and there are some
parts that have never even been flown over.

But change has come to the apparently changeless people
living in an unchanging land. The population has grown
beyond what the country can support, and the hungry ones

A muezzin on a minaret calls the faithful to prayer.

have moved out into the wider world. Around 3500 B.C., great waves of Arabs streamed across the intervening sands into the fertile valley of the Nile, and about the same time other waves covered the "land between the rivers," which we know as Mesopotamia. There have been other migrations before and since, but the greatest and most important was about thirteen hundred years ago, when the Arabs suddenly burst into history as world conquerors.

Within little more than a hundred years, they became the masters of an empire that stretched from the Atlantic Ocean to the borders of China. It was an empire far more extensive than the Romans had ruled at the height of their greatness. It included men of almost every race, creed, speech, and way of life. Nothing like it had been seen before, and there has been nothing to equal it since. And the most extraordinary thing about it is that it was all started by one man, and he a man who was born in a humble home, who had next to no education, few material advantages, and hardly anyone to help him. Indeed, for the greater part of his life, he lived in obscurity, looked down upon, laughed at. But something happened to him. In the last ten years of his life he became the master of Arabia, and, since his death, his power and influence have grown and grown. He is one of the really great figures of history. At the present time, several hundred millions of mankind—people with brown skins or black, yellow skins or white—hold him in the deepest reverence as the man above all men who was specially favored by God. They accept him not merely as a prophet but as *The Prophet*—the man chosen by God to preach the religion that has become one of the world's greatest religions and Christianity's chief competitor for the hearts and minds of men.

His name was Mohammed. That is how it is still usually spelled in English, although there is a tendency today to spell it Muhammad, which is a little nearer to the original pronunciation. Our grandfathers preferred Mahomet, but that form is seldom used nowadays.

The date of his birth is not certain, but it was probably A.D. 570. The place was Mecca, a small town about fifty miles inland from the Red Sea, in the part of Arabia called the Hijaz. His father's name was Abdallah, and his mother's Amina, and his family was one of the most highly regarded, although Abdallah himself was by no means wealthy. Like many of the Meccans, he was a merchant, who spent much of his time on trading expeditions to the surrounding countries. Soon after his marriage, he set off on one of these expeditions to Palestine, and on the return journey he was suddenly taken ill and died at Yathrib, or Medina, about 250 miles north of Mecca. Mohammed was born shortly afterward, so he never knew his father.

Nor could he have remembered very much about his mother. Amina was left to face the world with nothing more than five camels, a flock of goats, and a faithful Ethiopian slave girl named Baraka. Since the air of Mecca was considered unhealthy for children, she entrusted the little Mohammed to the care of a foster mother named Halima, who took him to live with her people—a tribe of Bedouins whose territory was in the neighborhood of the mountains of Taif. After five years, he was brought home, but very shortly thereafter, his mother died while on a visit to her husband's grave at Medina. The faithful slave girl took the little Mohammed back to Mecca, where she handed him over to his grandfather, Abd al-Mutallib. The old man made him welcome, for Abdallah had been his favorite son, and Mohammed spent two happy years under his grandfather's roof. Abd al-Mutallib was quite rich, and surrounded the little orphan with every comfort; but after about two years he too died, and Mohammed passed into the care of the eldest of his father's brothers, a man named Abu Talib.

As before, he was treated most kindly, but Abu Talib was poor and had a large family to support, and sometimes it was difficult to make ends meet. So Mohammed was given the job of looking after the sheep in the mountain pastures, and often had to pick berries for food. We are not told if he went to school: Very likely there was no school to go to. Some of his biographers have maintained that he never learned to read and write. But his uncle taught him to ride, to shoot with the bow, and to wield a sword, and he took him along on several of his trading expeditions, for he too was a merchant.

These journeys were the best part of Mohammed's education. The daily march across the sands, the halt at night at some lonely watering-hole, the tales told round the campfire of sprites and goblins and the ghosts of people who had lived long ago in the mysterious ruins that lay scattered about the desert—these things made a deep impression on the mind of a boy perhaps naturally given to melancholy. Then there were the people he met—traders like his uncle, soldiers, brigands, king's messengers, and preachers of strange religions.

Many legends have grown out of one of these personal contacts. It was with a Christian monk, variously named Sergius and Bahira, who had his hermit's cell near Bostra, a town to the east of the Jordan. The monk had seen many a caravan go by, and had given them hardly a glance. But now, he shouted across to Abu Talib's party and invited them to join in his frugal supper. They accepted, but left Mohammed behind in the camp to keep an eye on the camels and their stock in trade. The monk noticed that the boy was not there, however, and insisted that he should join them; according to the story, he had had a supernatural intimation that in this caravan there was a person who would become very important, and he suspected that the boy might well be that person. So Mohammed was sent for, and, when he had joined the others at the supper table, the monk watched him closely. After they had eaten, he took Mohammed aside and questioned him, and then asked him to take off his cloak so that he could see his back. The boy did so, and there between the shoulder blades was a mark rather like a mole, about the size of a pigeon's egg, which the monk recognized as a sign of a future prophet. When the time came to say goodbye, the monk told Abu Talib to keep an eye on his nephew, and look after him well, for he was destined to become a very great man. This strange incident is said to have been on Mohammed's first journey to Syria, when he was twelve years old.

The years passed, and Mohammed grew to manhood. He knew the life of the desert and had shared it, but he lived in a town, and that town the most important in the whole of northern Arabia. Mecca was situated in a barren, rocky valley with a harsh and unhealthy climate; in the summer the heat was almost unbearable. But through Mecca ran the "spice road," traveled by the caravans of traders and their animals coming fom the spice-producing countries of southern Arabia to sell their goods in the towns of Syria and beyond. It almost monopolized the trade between the Indian Ocean and the Mediterranean, and in its market place were bought and sold horses and camels, sheep and goats, cloaks, swords and spears, jewelry and precious stones, spices, foodstuffs in great variety, wool, hides and skins, and pearls from the offshore fisheries. It was also the principal slave mart for hundreds of miles around (as it still is), where Negroes who had been whisked across the Red Sea in Arab slavers were put up for auction on the slave block and sold to the highest bidder.

Furthermore, Mecca was a great religious center, for within its walls stood a temple that was holy to all the Arabian tribes. This structure was called the Kaaba, from the Arabic word for "cube," and in fact it was cube-shaped—an unpretentious, squat, and rather ugly building, originally roofless, in which were housed some hundreds of idols of the Arabian gods and goddesses. Embedded in a corner of the outer wall was a stone, which, it was believed, had been originally white when it "fell from Heaven," but in the course of ages had been blackened by the kisses of sinful men; very likely it was a meteorite. And close beside the Kaaba was a well called Zemzem, possibly from the noise that its water made as it bubbled up through the thirsty ground.

The Meccans were pagans. They worshiped the stars, the sun, the moon, and the planets Mercury, Venus, and Jupiter. Looking up at these heavenly bodies as they shone and sparkled in the night sky, they concluded, as so many other ancient peoples did, that in some mysterious fashion they influenced the lives and destinies of men. They also worshiped stones and trees and a great variety of other natural objects; furthermore, they paid reverence to the jinn, which were supposed to dwell in stones and trees and watch over wells and streams. Indeed, the Meccans saw gods and spirits everywhere, and one of the most thriving and profitable of the town's industries was the manufacture of idols, which were sold to the pilgrims who came to visit the Holy House of the Kaaba and to the Bedouin tribesmen who rode in occasionally from the desert to buy their few necessities and enjoy the rough and rude pleasures that the place afforded.

There was one god who was deemed to be superior to all the rest. His name was Allah. The holiest oaths were sworn by him, and covenants and treaties were sealed in his name. To call someone an enemy of Allah was to say the worst thing possible about him. Allah was too holy and mighty, however, to be approached by everyone on easy terms; much more accessible were the "daughters of Allah"—three goddesses whose names were Allat, Alozza, and Mana. Of the three, Allat was the most important; she has been identified with the great Mother Goddess who was worshiped throughout the Near East in ancient times. The center of her worship was

Taif, and sometimes she was held to be not Allah's daughter but his wife.

The Meccans loved their idols and thought of them not as mere blocks of carved wood or stone but as the tabernacles or dwelling places of the gods and angels, whose intercession with Allah they endeavored to obtain by means of sacrifices. Goats and camels were slain on stone altars, and the blood was smeared or splashed over the worshipers, who felt that in this way they became associated with the Divine and also became blood brothers, linked by the holiest and most unbreakable of ties. There is reason to believe that occasionally the Arabs offered up children on the altar of sacrifice.

Religion in Mecca was good for trade, and not only for the idol-makers. During four months of the year, there was a "holy truce," when military operations were suspended, raids on caravans were prohibited, and men involved in blood feuds had to keep their daggers sheathed. At these times, the tribesfolk for many miles around made their way to Mecca, where they walked or ran seven times round the Kaaba, offered the customary sacrifices, and made the expected gifts to the custodians of the shrine. Good business was done in the shops and bazaars, and when the bargaining had been completed, the visitors mingled with the townsmen and made merry in the wine bars and gambling dens.

Compared with the fine cities of the two great empires whose territories embraced Arabia at that time, Mecca was a poor place indeed. It was small, crowded, smelly, and shockingly dirty. Sanitation was nonexistent. There were no drains; no water supply other than wells that often ran dry and tanks that collected the water from the roofs after an all-too-infrequent storm. The diseases born of dirt and squalor took their endless toll. The houses were built of mud brick,

Mecca, Holy City of Islam. This view, based on the first photograph of the Holy City ever taken, shows the many-arched wall that surrounds the Great Mosque. The Kaaba, the cube-shaped building covered with a heavy carpet, dominates the courtyard, which is packed with pilgrims. The building with the pitched roof, in the immediate foreground, contains the well Zem-zem.

or plain mud, and they had flat mud roofs. Most of them consisted of one room, which was shared by the domestic animals, but the well-to-do citizen might have a house of several rooms on more than one floor. In these bigger houses, there was a central courtyard, where the porter slept at night among the camels.

Life in Mecca must have been full of interest and incident, however, notwithstanding the noise and discomfort, the dust and dirt and flies. Mohammed was more fortunate than most, for, although his uncle was comparatively poor, the tribe to which their family belonged was one of the most important and most highly respected in the place. It was known as the Koreish (Arabic *Quraysh*), and it included some of the

leading merchants. Moreover, the head of the Koreish was the
keeper of the Kaaba, who held the keys of the sanctuary and
had charge of its moneybags and treasure chest. The income
of the shrine was dispensed by this dignitary in defraying the
expenses of the poorer pilgrims and in giving a helping hand
to those who fell sick, were without friends, and had no means
to pay their passage home.

At Mecca, Mohammed must have met all classes and con-
ditions of men. Sitting beside his elders in the coffee shops,
he would hear strange tales of foreign parts; he would learn
something of politics, of class rivalries and struggles, of the
way in which the rich ground the faces of the poor. He would
meet free men and slaves, men of good character and dissolute
ne'er-do-wells, men who had risen to importance out of
nothing and men who had fallen from their high estate. The
inequalities of life, social injustice, political prejudice, the
shame of slavery, the subjection of women, cruelty to children
and animals, and the evils associated with what passed for
religion—they impressed him deeply. When, years later, he
had risen to power and greatness, he remembered these things,
the people he had met, the tales he had overheard or been
told.

But above all he was interested in the religions of the people
he encountered. When a caravan arrived from across the
desert, he was among the first to mix with the crowd that ran
to welcome the new arrivals. He listened eagerly to what the
travelers had to tell him of the beliefs and practices of their
homelands, and most of what they told him he stored up in
his retentive memory. Some of the visitors were Christians, he
learned, and soon he gathered that there were several different
kinds of Christians and they were usually at one another's
throats, although he found it quite beyond him to understand

the theological doctrines that distinguished them and kept them apart. Others were Jews, and he was particularly interested in what they had to tell him of the contents of their holy books. We can imagine him showing his friends the sights of the town, and his surprise when they seemed to know more about the Kaaba than he did. The original Kaaba had been built, it appeared, by Adam, the first man, and then, after this had been swept away in Noah's Flood, it had been rebuilt by the famous patriarch Abraham and his son Ishmael, from whom the Arabs claimed to be descended. The "Black Stone" hadn't really fallen from Heaven but had been brought down by the Angel Gabriel, who had handed it to Abraham and told him just where to place it in the wall. And the well Zem-zem—that was the very well that had suddenly gushed up in the desert when Ishmael and his mother Hagar were dying of thirst.

Mohammed listened to what the pilgrims had to say, and he could not help comparing their religions with the religion of the Meccans in which he had been brought up and which up to now he had thought must be true. He thought of the idols in the Kaaba, he thought of the idols that were part of the furnishings of every house, however humble. The Jews and Christians kept their thoughts about them to themselves, but, when he talked to them alone, he discovered that they had nothing but scorn for the gods of Arabia. They worshiped God, but their god was the One and Only God, or so they maintained: there was no other God but He. Might it be that this God of theirs was the Allah whom the Meccans and the whole world of Arabia worshiped, but that all the other gods and goddesses, spirits and *jinn*, whose images were to be found wherever you looked, were just *nothing?*

When he was about twenty, Mohammed served as a soldier

in a war that had broken out between the Koreish and another tribe in the neighborhood; we are told that he was present with his uncles in the battle that was fought, and discharged arrows at the enemy. But the campaign was soon over, and he returned to his humdrum life as a shepherd, day laborer, and camel-driver. Then, when he was twenty-five, he had a stroke of great good fortune. A wealthy widow, named Khadija, was looking for a thoroughly reliable and capable man to take charge of the trading caravans that she dispatched once a year to Aleppo and Damascus in Syria, and his uncle Abu Talib recommended Mohammed for the job. He jumped at the chance, and he carried out his duties to the widow's complete satisfaction. She was so impressed that she resolved to make him her husband. She had been twice widowed, and both her husbands had been rich men and had left their all to her, and by her skillful trading she had greatly increased her estate. She was therefore one of the richest ladies in Mecca. She was considerably older than Mohammed—about forty years to his twenty-five—but she was still beautiful. She felt herself falling in love with her handsome young business manager; and being a woman accustomed to having her own way, she employed a go-between to negotiate a match.

Mohammed raised no objection; on the contrary, he welcomed the proposal, and whether or not he loved her before their marriage he certainly did so afterward. And so they were married, and at once the young man who only a short time before had been a poor relation of Abu Talib's, with no fixed job and very uncertain prospects, was raised to a position of wealth and influence in his native city. No doubt there were women in Khadija's circle who held up their hands in surprise that she should so demean herself as to marry, after two such wealthy spouses, a man who had been a camel-driver, but they had to admit that Mohammed made a very handsome husband. Tradition speaks of his commanding presence, his majestic aspect, his piercing black eyes, jet-black hair and beard, his gracious smile, and grave and courteous demeanor.

Notwithstanding the great difference in their ages and social position, the union of Mohammed and Khadija turned out to be a very happy one. Six children were born to them, two boys and four girls. The boys died in infancy, but the girls grew up and were found husbands in due course.

For several years after his marriage, Mohammed continued as his wife's business manager and was kept busy. He visited the great Arabian fairs, and sometimes accompanied the caravans to more distant parts. He mixed on equal terms with the city elders, and had his place in the council that managed the affairs of the town and of the Kaaba.

As time went on, however, there was less need for him to busy himself in the actual running of the business. He and his wife already had as much wealth as they wanted, and they had no sons to provide for. So, more and more, he was able to delegate his responsibilities, and found time to indulge his turn for reverie and religious speculation. He withdrew from Mecca whenever he could, and retired to the desert, where he spent days and nights out there in the great open spaces, alone with himself and the stars. Sometimes, however, Khadija went with him, and Mohammed was glad. Even though she was not able to share in the thoughts that increasingly worried him, she was able to sympathize, and to Mohammed her tender sympathy was very precious.

2

The Persecuted Prophet

More and more, Mohammed grew dissatisfied with the religion of the Meccans. The manner in which they mixed piety with profit disgusted him. He deplored the way in which poor pilgrims were fleeced by the innkeepers and the custodians of the Kaaba and the Sacred Stone. He was angry when he saw the wine bars crowded with drunken revelers, the gaming dens packed with gamblers, the haunts of the lowest forms of vice filled with pilgrims who, when they took the homeward way, would be leaving behind them their money and their health, their reputation and any ideas of godliness that might have inspired them when they arrived. He glanced with increasing scorn at the idols that crammed the Kaaba and its precincts, and his indignation mounted when he saw the tradesmen parceling out the images of wood and stone which, so they assured their simple-minded customers, were gods and goddesses that really could work wonders.

Whenever he could, he entered into conversation with men of other faiths. He invited them to his home, and they talked together long into the night. Then, a cousin of his wife, a man named Waraka who had become a Christian and was familiar with the Bible, introduced him to some good people who did not profess any particular religion or creed but called themselves *Hanifs*, or "penitents." Like him, these people were disgusted with the get-rich-quick paganism of Mecca; they scoffed at the images and superstitious practices of their fellow citizens—but only when the door was shut and the windows closed, for fear that they might be overheard. They talked things over among themselves, compared experiences, tried to find out what was right and then set out to do it. They believed in Allah, and only in Allah; and to do His will was for them the one thing necessary, the most terribly important thing in all the world. Mohammed learned a great deal from the Hanifs.

In the course of his lonely rambles he had come across a cave on Mount Hira, about 9 miles north of Mecca, and there he would go, whenever he could get away from business, and would spend days and nights, engaged in prayer and meditation. For days, he would go without food and drink, and, at night, instead of sleeping, he would roam about the sands, look up at the stars, and wonder. He heard mysterious voices; he had strange visions. Sometimes he was seized with a violent trembling, and then swooned or fell into convulsions. Perspiration would stream down his face in even the coldest weather. He would lie with his eyes closed, foaming at the mouth and making grunting or bellowing noises.

Khadija was deeply worried about him, but she was always

ready to cheer and comfort. Slowly he came to the conclusion
that he was not as other men. Allah had picked him out for
some great work, and he trembled at the thought. He had
been poor; he was uneducated; he felt himself unworthy. Yet
was it just a silly delusion on his part that Allah had chosen
him to be a *prophet?*

One night (in the month of Ramadan, the holy month of
the Arabs, which he now always spent in the desert), he was
in the cavern at Hira, alone, when something extraordinarily
strange happened to him. On the horizon, he saw a tremendous figure, like a man, but ever so much bigger and more
splendid than any man he knew. The figure began to move
toward him, came nearer and nearer, until there was only the
distance of two bow shots between them. And then (in his
dream or vision, sleeping or awake), he saw that it was an
angel holding in his hand a silken cloth on which appeared
what seemed to be writing. And now the angel spoke. "Read!"
he commanded.

"But I can't," murmured Mohammed shakily; "I don't
know how to."

Again the angel spoke. "Read!" and again, and yet again.
At last, Mohammed managed to stammer, "What shall I
read?" And this is what, years afterward, he said the angel
told him to say:

"Read"—or perhaps the word is better rendered, "Recite"
—"Recite in the name of the Lord, Who has created all
things, Who created man out of a clot of blood. Recite! In
the name of the Most High. Who hath taught man the use of
the pen, Who teaches man what he did not know. . . ."

When he came to himself, Mohammed found the words
"engraved on his heart" as he put it. He could not forget
them, nor could he understand what they meant. Had he

dreamed it all, or was he possessed by an evil spirit? The more he thought about it, the more depressed he became, and he even contemplated suicide. But, just as he was about to throw himself over a precipice, he felt hands holding him back. Filled with horror, trembling with fright, he hurried away from the spot, but had not gone far when he heard the voice again, calling him back. This time it seemed to come from Heaven; there was nothing terrible about it, rather it was warm and soothing, and charged with encouragement. "Oh Mohammed," it said, "I am Gabriel, the angel of Allah, and you—you are indeed the Prophet [or Apostle] of Allah!" And as he described it long afterward, "that night there was peace, until the break of dawn."

The Prophet had received his "call." In years to come, his followers came to refer to the occasion as the "Night of Power," and fixed it toward the end of the month of Ramadan (A.D. 610).

Meanwhile, Khadija had been getting very anxious, and had sent out messengers to see what had become of him. They failed to find him, and she feared that he had suffered some grievous mishap, been killed by a wild beast perhaps. But, later in the day, he came striding home, and he could hardly wait to tell Khadija all the wonderful things that had happened to him. To his great relief, she listened understandingly. She never doubted for a moment the truth of what he told her. "Of course you are the Apostle of Allah," we can imagine her saying; "I've known it all along." When he still seemed to be rather downcast, she bade him rejoice. "Don't think for a moment that Allah will bring you to shame," she declared. "Haven't you been a good kinsman to your relations, kind to your neighbors, charitable to the poor, hospitable to the stranger, faithful to your word, and ever a defender of what you believed to be the truth?" Profoundly moved, Mohammed welcomed his wife as his first convert.

Yes, he was a prophet, Allah's chosen messenger, and now he set about telling the great news to others. For a time, he confined his revelations to his own household. After Khadija, the first to avow himself a believer in Mohammed's mission was his servant Zayd, an Arab who had once been his slave but whom he had liberated and treated like a son. About the same time he was joined by his cousin Ali (the son of his uncle Abu Talib), who was then a boy of about ten, or perhaps a little older, and was living in Mohammed's house as his adopted son in place of Mohammed's own sons who had died. It was at a family gathering, called by Mohammed to proclaim his mission, that Ali made his decision, and his elders were greatly amused when he boldly accepted Mohammed's invitation to become his brother, his lieutenant, his vizier. Mohammed looked round the circle of unsympathetic faces, and then flung his arms around the generous-minded boy. "Behold my lieutenant, my vizier!" he cried; "let all of you listen to his words and obey him." But they only laughed, and no one else joined him on this occasion.

The next recruit was his friend Abu Bakr, a man about two years his junior, a merchant, and a genial, sympathetic soul who was also possessed of sound common sense and a good measure of practical ability. Others came along as time passed, but progress was distressingly slow. In the first three years of the Prophet's mission, the number of converts did not exceed forty, and these for the most part were young people who were as yet of no consequence in the world, slaves, and strangers to the city who had found in Mohammed a friend. They met whenever they could to pray together and to hear Mohammed preach at a private house or in a cavern in the hills outside the city. Even so, news of their activities reached the ears of the chiefs of the Koreish, and there was trouble. At first, his fellow citizens laughed at Mohammed. "The fellow's gone crazy," they said; "he sees visions and hears voices, he falls into fits, and obviously he's a very sick man." But when, not content with declaring himself to be a prophet, Mohammed made open attacks on the established religion of the place, they were absolutely furious. So Mohammed wanted to abolish idol-worship, did he? And idol-making was such a thriving industry! He complained of the goings-on at the fairs and religious festivals: well, perhaps they were a bit shocking at times—but then, they were so good for trade! He said that the Black Stone was only a piece of rock, that the images were nothing more than things of wood and stone made by men's hands and had nothing of the Divine about them, that there was only one god, and that was Allah! He believed in Allah— well, that was something to his credit, at least; but they had a shrewd suspicion that when he spoke of Allah, it wasn't the sort of Allah they had in mind.

For nine years, the Prophet preached. His sermons were short and simple. "There is only one god, Allah, and Mohammed is the Apostle of Allah!" In his own house, and in a friend's house, and in the Kaaba itself, he proclaimed his message, and he made many more enemies than converts. All the same, his progress was sufficient to arouse the nervous fears of the city rulers. Some of them went to Abu Talib and told him that he ought to keep his nephew in order. Abu Talib was probably concerned for Mohammed's safety, and urged him to restrain his enthusiasm. "Spare your remonstrances, Uncle," rejoined Mohammed; "even if they placed the sun on my right hand and the moon on my left, to turn me from my undertaking, I would not pause for a moment. The Lord will carry me to victory, or I will die in the attempt."

Abu Talib probably thought his nephew was demented, but he admired his courage. Moreover, he was an Arab, and, among the Arabs, family feeling is sacred. He continued to give him his protection, not without some risk to himself, and, as long as Abu Talib was alive, Mohammed was exposed to nothing worse than pinpricks, petty insults, and personal boycott. He was a man apart, one whom it was considered dangerous to know and to be seen with.

Far worse was the experience of his humble converts. They had no powerful protector, and Mohammed himself could do little to help them. They were persecuted, put in chains, imprisoned, and sometimes whipped. At length, their position grew so miserable that the Prophet advised such of them as could to get away and seek a new home across the Red Sea in Abyssinia. The Christian king of that country received the migrants kindly, but they were homesick, and when, after about a year, they heard that Mohammed had made his peace with the Koreish, they lost no time in hurrying home.

What had happened was this. Mohammed was in the Kaaba one day, sitting alone, sunk in despondency. Things seemed to be so hopeless. For years, he had preached and prayed and protested, and what had he to show for all his efforts? Still the number of converts was only about fifty. The scorn and malice of his opponents were as bitter as ever; and what had he to look forward to but a long period of continued opposition, scoffing and insult, and perhaps in the end complete failure?

Suddenly he broke his silence, and those sitting within earshot thought they heard him say something to the effect that, after all, the three goddesses, the 'daughters of Allah," whose images stood in the place of honor in front of where they were sitting, might perhaps have some power of intercession with Allah!

The idolators were pleasantly surprised. The so-called prophet had confessed his error. They no longer had to be afraid of what he would do if he ever had the power to overthrow their idols and put an end to the profitable pilgrimages to the pagan shrine! A reconciliation seemed possible, and, for the first time in years, they gave Mohammed a smile and a word of friendly greeting.

Perhaps it was those condescending glances that shocked Mohammed into a realization of what he had done. Almost at once, he bitterly regretted the concession he had made in a moment of weakness, and he took the first opportunity of repairing his mistake. Towering above them in indignation, he pointed contemptuously at the images and exclaimed, "Allat and Alozza and Mana—what do you think they are? I will tell you. They are just empty names! And you and your forefathers have called them goddesses!"

The people howled against him, spat at him, and shook their fists in his face, and, but for his uncle's protecting arm, they would have stoned him for blasphemy. The more angry they became, the more Mohammed was convinced that he had done right. Henceforth, he would refuse to compromise. He had burned his bridges, and it was now a fight to a finish. The converts, who had returned so hopefully from Abyssinia, hastened to go back there, and with them went a number more—about a hundred souls all told. Mohammed stayed behind in Mecca, and he was greatly cheered when he was joined by some bold spirits who admired his pluck and constancy. Among these was a man named Umar, who was destined to a great future as the Prophet's lieutenant.

By preaching and personal conversation, the Prophet continued his work, and he also continued to experience, in these critical days, revelations that he believed were sent to him from Heaven. As they fell from his lips, in moments of trance or when he had freshly awakened from dream-filled sleep, they were written down by his scribes or secretaries. Eventually, years later, they became incorporated in the book that is known as the Koran.

One of the revelations must have greatly mystified his hearers, as it has mystified all the commentators ever since. "Praise be unto Allah," it runs, "who transported his servant from the sacred temple [at Mecca] to the farther temple [supposed to be at Jerusalem]." This simple statement has been elaborated into a wonderful story of Mohammed being carried through the air in an instant, on a supernatural steed called al-Borak ("lightning"), from Mecca to Jerusalem, where he met Abraham, Moses, Jesus, and other prophets, and thence to the "seventh heaven," where he was actually touched by the finger of Allah. Very likely, the basis of this was only a dream, and the Prophet cannot be held responsible for the absurd details. It is the only miraculous incident of any importance associated with him.

But now Abu Talib died, and also, a little earlier or a little later—the records are inconclusive—the ever faithful Khadija. Abu Talib had lived a pagan, and he died a pagan, but he had never swerved from what he conceived to be his duty to protect his nephew in accordance with the immemorial Arab custom. As soon as he was gone, Mohammed's enemies intensified their hostility, and it was clear that they would do their best to get rid of him.

Mohammed felt his uncle's death keenly, but the loss of Khadija struck him to the heart. Their marriage had been a very happy one, notwithstanding the differences in age and social condition, and it is significant that, although polygamy was customary in Arabia and he himself believed and taught that it was sanctioned by Allah, he took no second wife as long as Khadija was alive. Nor did he ever give her the slightest cause for jealousy. He lamented her passing deeply, and he remembered her with affection and gratitude to the day of his death. She had been his first convert. She had been always ready to listen to him, she had always believed in him and his message, she was the mother of his children, and his unfailing friend.

Before long he married again, and, indeed, he became the master of a large harem. But not even the favorite wife of his later years could supplant Khadija in his affections. One day this radiant young woman (her name was Ayesha, and she was the daughter of Abu Bakr) asked him about Khadija. "She was a widow, wasn't she?" she demanded; "she was old and had lost her looks. You love me better than you loved her, don't you?" And Mohammed (so the story goes) replied, "No, no! A thousand times no! There can never be a better woman than she was. When I was poor, she brought me riches. She believed in me when no one else would believe. In the whole world I had only one friend, and she was that!"

Now that Abu Talib was no longer there to protect him, the Meccans did their best to render Mohammed's life miserable and intolerable. The head of the Koreish was now another uncle, one Abu Lahab, and he was the Prophet's bitter enemy. It was a critical period, probably the most critical in Mohammed's career, and he found it advisable to leave Mecca for a time. With his faithful Zayd, he moved to Taif, some 70 miles from Mecca, where he may have hoped to spend some time in peaceful retirement. But the place was a hotbed

of idolatry, and, when he saw the crowds prostrating themselves before the image of the goddess Allat, the Prophet could
not restrain himself. For ten days, he preached to unwilling
ears, and then the populace, egged on by the chiefs and elders,
violently assaulted him and his companion. Wounded, covered
with blood, their very lives in peril, the two managed to escape
to the surrounding hills, where they found shelter among the
vineyards that covered the slopes. After a few days, they made
their way back to Mecca, and the old dreary round of hostility and hate began again.

Suddenly the tide turned. The season of the annual pilgrimage had come round, and the Prophet had ventured forth to
preach to the assembled crowds. He was walking outside the
city when he happened to meet six pilgrims who, it turned out,
had come from Medina (or Yathrib, as it was called in those
days). They began talking, and he explained to them his
teaching. They were impressed by his personality, listened
intently, and then, to his great joy, said that they were will-
ing to accept what he told them. Now the conversation
shifted to Mohammed's present plight: perhaps, he ventured
to suggest, things might be better for him in Medina. They
fingered their beards, and promised to think the matter over.
They would be coming to the pilgrimage again next year,
they said, and would let him know then.

They did not know, and he did not know, that this brief
encounter in the summer of A.D. 620 would be of immense
importance in the history of the world.

The year passed, and again the pilgrims swarmed about the
Kaaba.

We can imagine Mohammed's impatience as he looked for
the promised visitors. He need not have worried. Five of the
six had come, and they had brought seven more with them.

They also brought good news. Medina (they told him) was in a state of constant turmoil; rival families kept the place in an uproar with their feuds, and the mass of the people wanted nothing so much as a man strong enough to knock their heads together and make them keep the peace. As for Mohammed's teaching, they were quite prepared to give it a fair hearing.

Thereupon, on the hill of Akaba, just outside Mecca, the twelve men from Medina swore a solemn oath that, henceforth, they would renounce idolatry and have no other god but Allah, that they would act justly and keep themselves from immorality, that they would not kill their unwanted children "as the pagan Arabs do," and that they would obey the Prophet in all things lawful.

Mohammed gripped their hands as they promised fidelity, and, when he said good-by, sent back with them one of his followers, who would instruct them more fully in the faith of Islam, as their new religion was called. Henceforth, they would be known as Muslims.

Another year went by, and again it was the season of pilgrimage. Again, a band of Medinans came to greet Mohammed, and this time they numbered about seventy. He listened eagerly to what they had to tell him. The idols had been thrown down, quite a number of the people had embraced Islam, and many more were only awaiting the opportunity. They were ready to receive him. Would he come?

Mohammed cannot have thought the matter over very long. For years, he had encountered the Meccans' hostility. They had rejected him and his message. After years of preaching, the converts to Islam were but a handful, and the future looked dark. And now these men had come from a distant city, and had made him an offer that was generous indeed. The Meccans had denounced him as mad; they had called him a liar, an impostor, a cheat. The Medinans were ready to receive him as their teacher and as a kind of referee in their political disputes. Who knew what it might lead to?

Toward the close of the pilgrimage, the envoys went to the hill of Akaba, where it had been arranged that they should meet the Prophet and receive his answer. Mohammed did not join them until midnight, for he wanted to keep the matter from the ears of his enemies, and he took with him his uncle Abbas.

Abbas was not a believer in his nephew's teaching, but his sense of Arab loyalty made him urge the men from Medina to neither raise hopes that they might not be able to fulfill nor promise a protection that they could not really guarantee. The Medinans replied that they felt quite confident that they could secure Mohammed's safety, and that of as many friends as wanted to accompany him. Furthermore, they were fully prepared to accept him as their Prophet. Abbas was satisfied, and so was Mohammed. He swore to be faithful to them, as they had sworn to be faithful to him.

"Henceforth," he assured the Medinans, "I am your friend, and your enemies are my enemies." "But," inquired one nervous questioner, "supposing we happen to get killed in your service, what will be our reward?" The Prophet replied in one word: "Paradise." The Medinans were content. Again they pledged their faith, and then took the homeward road, while he went back to Mecca to complete his preparations for joining them.

In the next few weeks, most of Mohammed's supporters managed to slip out of Mecca and made for Medina. They left mostly at night and with a minimum of fuss, but the sight of their empty homes gave the rulers of the city an inkling of what was going on. They were concerned at the loss of so

Muslims leave the mosque of El Muayyad in Cairo after Friday prayers. This mosque has two minarets, which rise above the Gate of Bab Zuweila.

much useful manpower, the more so since their loss was a
rival city's gain. But what worried them far more was their
inability to understand just what Mohammed was up to. The
man was a nuisance, and had been for a long time; on the one
hand, they would be very glad to get rid of him, but, on the
other, they suspected that, once he had gotten away from
Mecca, he might be an even greater nuisance. What was he
going to do in Medina? What was his position going to be?
Suppose—just suppose—the outcast from Mecca became the
chief of the city situated right across the route to the north
that must be followed by all the Meccan caravans?

As things turned out, they had good cause to be worried.
But there seemed to be little they could do about it beyond
keeping a careful watch on Mohammed. Very likely, they
planned to have him arrested on some trumped-up charge of
treachery if he, too, should show signs of taking the road to
the north.

Now, all the Muslims had gone except Abu Bakr, Ali, and
Mohammed himself. The day fixed for their departure was
imminent, and news reached the Prophet that his enemies
were looking for him, to make sure that he was still there.
Hurriedly he told Ali to get into his bed, and threw over the
youth his own red mantle, while he slipped away over the
garden wall to Abu Bakr's house. When the spies of the
Koreish peeped through a crack in Mohammed's door, they
saw a man in bed whom they took to be Mohammed, and
reported accordingly to their masters.

Meanwhile, Mohammed and Abu Bakr were making their
escape. First they made for a cave on Mount Thaur, some 6
miles to the *south* of Mecca, the opposite direction to the one
they might be expected to take. There they remained in hid-
ing for three days. Food was brought them by Abdallah and

Asma, Abu Bakr's son and daughter, and a faithful shepherd kept them supplied with milk.

Very soon their flight had become known, and everywhere men were looking for them. The pursuit was hot, and several times they were very nearly caught. The piety of later days has embroidered the tale with incidents of a miraculous character: a spider spun its web over the mouth of the cave, which was further blocked by a tree that suddenly sprang up and whose branches contained a nest in which two pigeons laid their eggs; the searchers were struck blind as they were getting inconveniently close. . . . We may assume that something distracted the pursuers' attention from the cave entrance at the critical moment.

At nightfall, the two fugitives left the cave and sought a breath of air outside. One night, even Abu Bakr's stout heart began to fail him. How easy it would be for an assassin to conceal himself among the rocks! Even now, behind that bush over there, he might be stringing his arrow or raising his spear! "There are such a lot of them against us," he murmured to his master, "and only two of us!" Mohammed was undaunted. "You are wrong, Abu Bakr," he rejoined; "there are two of us, true enough, but in our midst is God, Who makes a third!"

On the fourth day after leaving home, they collected two camels that Abu Bakr had arranged should be in readiness at a certain spot, and struck off westward across the desert to near the Red Sea, thus bypassing Mecca. On the eighth day, they looked down from the hills on the oasis of Medina, and it must have seemed delightful, with its fields and orchards and palm groves—an island of peace and plenty in a troubled world. A few hours later, they were passing through the city gate, and their friends were there to greet them. Tired and travel-stained, the Prophet and his faithful lieutenant got down stiffly from their camels, and partook of the refreshment that was bountifully provided.

Within a few weeks, they were joined by Ali and the members of their households who had been left behind in Mecca, but who were allowed to leave at their leisure and without molestation.

3

The Prince of Medina

Mohammed's migration from Mecca to Medina is called "the Hegira." The word comes from the Arabic *hijra*, which is usually translated "flight." But perhaps a better rendering is "the breaking of old ties, a new departure, a fresh start." And that is what it was. It marked the beginning of a new era in the history of a large part of the world.

Very much as the Christian Era is dated from the birth of Christ, so the Mohammedan, or Islamic, Era is dated from the Hegira. The actual day on which the Prophet arrived at Medina was probably September 24, but the Mohammedan Era starts from the first day of the year in which the Hegira took place, i.e., our July 16, 622. From the first, the importance of the move was recognized, and the decision to make it the start of a new calendar was taken within a generation or so after Mohammed's death.

33

At the time, the Prophet was a man in his early fifties, when most men would think twice about taking on new responsibilities. But before him lay ten years of tremendous activity and achievement.

In the early months of his life in Medina, Mohammed was in the position of a religious leader who had been called in to tackle a political problem. The people, or most of them, were ready to give him a fair trial. They let him do what he liked with their idols, presumably because they had already lost trust in them, and they even agreed to accept Mohammed as their Prophet. His power was by no means absolute, however, and there were men who would have been only too pleased if he made a wrong move. But, however uncompromising he was in matters of religion, in affairs of state he could be tactful and accommodating.

He demonstrated this soon after his arrival. He had to choose a site for his house and for the religious building—the mosque—that was to stand beside it. Where should it be? Some of his supporters wanted it to be in *their* quarter of the town, others with just as good a claim to his consideration wanted it to be in *theirs*. The Prophet pondered, and then he let his camel decide. He rode it through the town, and, where it stopped, there he ordered the builders to set to work. The site happened to be the property of two orphans, and he was careful to pay the full market price for it. And the house that he built was not a palace but a commonplace dwelling such as many a Medinan would have disdained to live in. His way of life turned out to be just as simple. He hated show and despised luxury. When he preached in the weekly assembly, he stood facing the congregation with his back against a palm tree, and it was years before he could be persuaded to indulge in the use of a chair. When they made a pulpit for him, he insisted that it should be of plain wood.

On the whole, he made an excellent impression. Obviously, he was a strong character, and that is what they wanted—a man strong enough to establish law and order after the years of dismal conflict. As we have noted, there was a hard core of pagans who were not at all keen on accepting his rule, even as an impartial referee in their disputes, but there was another and more important section of the population that stood aloof. These were the Jews—that is, the Arabs who had embraced Judaism as their religion. They seem to have been numerous in Medina and its environs, and to have been wealthy. Mohammed tried his best to secure their allegiance. "After all," he may have reasoned, "they are monotheists, believers in One God just as Muslims are, even though they call Him Jehovah and we call Him Allah." When he came to institute one day of the week on which there should be public prayers in the mosque, he settled on Friday, on which day the Jewish sabbath begins. Furthermore, he ordered the Muslims to turn in the direction of Jerusalem, the holy city of the Jews, when they prayed. He did his best to conciliate the Jews, and he must have been very much distressed when they declined his friendly advances.

Before long, the suspicions had turned into open quarreling, but Mohammed had his hands full. There was a question of immediate importance that had to be settled: How were he and his followers who had reached Medina from Mecca to live? Up to now, they had been dependent on the hospitality of the Muslims in Medina, but obviously that could not go on forever. There were no vacant lands in the neighborhood to be farmed. Medina had already more than enough tradesmen, craftsmen, and men engaged in commerce. How, then, were they to live?

Mohammed cannot have been in much doubt about the answer. There was really no alternative to the course of action that he must have thought out before he left Mecca, and that was the traditional Arabian activity of caravan-raiding.

The idea was to take a small party of unfriendly tribesmen by surprise and make off with their camels and provisions, and perhaps a pretty girl who took the raiders' fancy. The aim was not to kill but to rob.

So Mohammed turned to raiding as a means of livelihood, and the Meccan caravans must have seemed a godsend. Not only were the Meccans his enemies, but they were pagans and enemies of Allah. From the smallness of the numbers engaged, it seems clear that initially he had to rely entirely on his own companions. Week after week, the Muslim parties lay in wait, but nothing came their way. When they did strike, it was only a minor affair: six Muslims attacked a party of four Meccans, killed one, took two prisoners, and let the fourth man go to tell the tale. But it occurred in one of the sacred months, when the time-honored custom was that there should be no bloodshed. The chiefs of the Koreish were shocked when they heard of it, and so must have been many of the Medinans. But it had been successful, and Mohammed silenced the doubters with the pronouncement that henceforth there would be no sympathy for infidels. So the Meccans and the whole tribe of idolaters knew what to expect.

The next engagement was far more serious. A force of about 300 Muslims, including this time some 60 Medinans, under the leadership of Mohammed himself, set out to intercept a rich caravan that was returning to Mecca from Syria. Its leader, however, learned of the affair and took another road, while also sending an express messenger to Mecca to summon reinforcements. To his chagrin, the Prophet found that the caravan had slipped from his grasp and that he was confronted by a force of more than twice his strength. Willingly or unwillingly, he stayed to fight, and, at daybreak on a day in March, 624, the battle began.

It was an intensely hot day, and both sides suffered terribly from thirst. The Meccans had less discipline and water, and, at the critical moment Mohammed jumped down from the stand from which he had been watching the fight and led the final charge himself. "Let their faces be covered with confusion!" he shouted, and the Meccans wavered and fled. Seventy of their number were slain and seven taken prisoner, while Mohammed's losses were fourteen all told. In the hour of victory some of the prisoners were butchered, but the Prophet stayed the slaughter with the reminder that his followers had left their wives and children in Mecca at the mercy of their foes. The rest of the prisoners were ransomed, and this made up in some measure for the loss of the caravan, which, in the excitement of the moment, had slipped away. The Muslim dead were buried with full military honors on the battlefield, and it is said that their grave is honored to this day.

So ended what is called the Battle of Badr. The numbers involved were so insignificant that it may seem out of place to call it a battle. And yet it has been ranked among the decisive battles of the world. It was the first name on the battle-roll of Islam. The Prophet had drawn the sword, and henceforth the progress of Islam would depend on naked valor.

Not long afterward, a second battle was fought—on Mount Uhud, 6 miles north of Medina. The Meccans had brought into the field a force of 3,000 men, including 200 horsemen,

and 3,000 camels; Mohammed had practically no horses, and
950 men at most. In the opening charge, the Muslims were
successful, and the invaders gave way. Their retreat became
a rout, and their women fled screaming from their tents as
the victors swarmed over the camp and began to ravage and
plunder. But a Meccan captain, a man named Khalid—whom
we shall meet again—seized the opportunity and charged the
disordered Muslims from the rear with his cavalry. It was the
Muslims' turn to flee. The Prophet was wounded in the face
with a javelin and lost several teeth; the rumor spread that he
was dead, but his followers had dragged him away to a neigh-
boring ditch, where he lay concealed until he could be carried
off the field. Seventy Muslims were killed, and the Meccan
loss was a mere twenty-seven. Fortunately, the Meccans
thought that they had done well enough for one day, and
they failed to follow up their success. In the morning, Mohammed, able to ride a horse again, led his little army out in
front of Medina and boldly challenged the enemy to renew
the fight. But the Meccans only shook their spears in defiance
and made their way home.

Uhud might well have been the end of Mohammed—and
of Islam. But, in fact, the Prophet's prestige was enhanced,
since it was against his orders that the Medinans had started
to plunder the enemy camp. Henceforth, the Prophet could
rely not only on his Muslims but on the whole strength of
Medina. He had begun as a religious leader and as an impartial
referee; now, he was recognized as the military commander
and political chief. He was indeed the Prince of Medina.

In 627, the Meccans, in company with their allies among
the Bedouin tribes, attacked Medina again, and, to their dis-
gust, the Prophet refused to come out into the open to meet
them but dug a deep ditch around the place, which they were

unable to cross. After nearly three weeks of ineffectual skirmishing and shouting of insults, their supplies ran out, and they had to retreat once more. They must have thought the ditch most unsportsmanlike.

It was following this "Battle of the Ditch" that there occurred the episode that has left the darkest stain on Mohammed's name. The Jewish tribe of Koraiza deserted his alliance at the most critical moment, and, in the hour of victory, he resolved to make an example of them. He led his troops against their castle and compelled them to surrender unconditionally. For some reason, he left their fate to be decided by the chief of another tribe of Jews, which had remained loyal to their alliance, and this man adjudged that the men should be put to death and the women and children sold into slavery! The shameful verdict was approved by the Prophet, and the unhappy Jews, numbering some 800, were led out, in batches of five or six, and beheaded in the market place on the edge of a trench into which their bodies were thrown. It is on record that only one Jew saved his life by abjuring his religion, and it is also recorded that a Jewish merchant put in a successful bid for some of the women and children. The homes and other possessions of the victims were distributed among Mohammed's landless followers.

It is a shocking story, but it should be remembered that, in the Arabia of that time, when tribes went to war, they felt no obligations toward one another. The enemy had no rights whatsoever. They were men outside the pale, and not even the rules of what might be considered common decency compelled any restraint. The only thing that kept men from killing indiscriminately and being even more cruel and savage than they were was the fear of retaliation by the next of kin, the bloodbrothers, of the murdered.

While nothing can clear this stain from Mohammed's reputation, it should also be recognized that, as soon as he was able, he instituted a new and higher morality that embraced all Muslims—whatever their tribe and race, country and color—in one great Brotherhood of Islam. As we shall learn, his last great sermon was devoted to this noble theme.

Back in Medina, the people thought no less of him because of his brutality. On the contrary, they felt that a man who could do such great things as defeating the Meccans and suppressing the Jews was worthy of their wholehearted allegiance. There were no critics of his rule now. Everyone accepted him as the Prophet and also as Prince. Originally, he had come among them as the preacher of a new religion; now the religion had become the state. A new political power had arisen in the world. Gone forever was the attempt to conciliate the opposition—the Jews in particular. The edict that the faithful should turn toward Jerusalem in their prayers was rescinded; henceforth, the direction should be that of Mecca. The Prophet even ventured to interfere with the long-established habits of the people, as when he insisted that indulgence in strong drink be banned.

It was about this time that the city, which had been known since time immemorial as Yathrib, was given the new name of Medina, "City of Cities" or "The City" (i.e., of the Prophet), by which name it has been known ever since.

By the free choice of an independent people, the fugitive from Mecca had been raised to the position of a prince, with thousands of bold and eager men to do his bidding. Each year that went by saw an increase in his fighting strength, and, while at first his army was employed only against Arab tribes and Jewish colonists who were slow to acknowledge his rule and the supremacy of Allah, it was obviously only a matter of time before it was launched against more important foes.

It was in A.D. 628 that the Prophet is thought to have dispatched letters to the great potentates that he had heard of, demanding that they should abandon their false worships and adopt the faith of Islam. The Negus or King of Abyssinia is supposed to have received such a letter, and also the King of Persia, Chosroes II, and the Emperor Heraclius, who ruled the East Roman or Byzantine Empire from his great capital city of Constantinople. The Persian is said to have torn the missive to pieces in a rage, but the Roman Emperor received his courteously, probably thinking that it came from a harmless fanatic. The Roman governor of Egypt was even more considerate, doubtless because he was anxious to keep on good terms with the Arab tribes that bordered his province. He treated Mohammed's envoys with great honor, we are told, and sent presents of a white mule and two Coptic slave girls, one of whom, known as Mary the Egyptian, was so beautiful that she caused a good deal of jealousy among the other women of the Prophet's harem.

Whether or not the Emperor and kings received Mohammed's sublimely audacious letters, whether or not the letters were sent, there is no doubt that similar letters were dispatched to the Arabian sheiks. Some of the replies were considered insufficiently precise, and the Muslim armies were set in motion to secure a more suitable response. So began the holy war of Islam against idolaters, unbelievers, and believers in other faiths, including the "people of the Book," as the Jews and Christians were called. They were offered a choice among three alternatives: acceptance of Islam, death, or the payment of a special tax. Fortunately, perhaps, for the Muslim economic system, great numbers in all the countries invaded by the Muslim armies chose the last.

All Mohammed's teaching was well calculated to inspire his followers to do and dare. He held out before them a dazzling prospect of piety and plunder. The pagan Arabs had the haziest notions about any afterlife, but Mohammed described the joys of Heaven and the pains of Hell in the most vivid fashion. "The sword," he declared, "is the key of Heaven. A drop of blood shed in the cause of Allah counts for more than two months of fasting and prayer. Whosoever falls in battle, his sins are forgiven, and at the Day of Judgment the limbs he has lost will be replaced by angels' wings." Furthermore, his doctrine made for a fatalistic attitude. Nothing happens save by the will of Allah; if it is a man's destiny to die on the battlefield, then he will die there, but if otherwise, then he will pass unharmed through storms of darts and arrows.

Added to these powerful inducements was something that made the strongest appeal to freebooters among the Arabs— the promise of heaps of plunder. All the possessions of the defeated were to be seized as a matter of course in the day of victory; a fifth of the spoils was specially reserved to the Prophet, to be applied to religious and charitable purposes, and the rest was to be divided among the men who had fought and the dependents of the fallen. It is not surprising that, with so many inducements, the soldiers of Mohammed carried his white banner to triumph on countless hard-fought fields.

At last, after he had been in Medina for seven or eight years, the Prophet felt that he was strong enough to make a direct thrust at Mecca. It was his birthplace, the home of his ancestors, and, notwithstanding the treatment that its rulers had extended toward him, he still felt a deep affection for the place. In some strange, indefinable way, Mecca was the heart and soul of Arabia, and the Prophet was resolved to make it his, and Allah's, before he died. In A.D. 628, he marched on Mecca at the head of a caravan of 1,500 men, with the expressed intention of making the pilgrimage. He arrived within two days' journey of the city, but was then faced by such a show of force that he had to resort to diplomacy rather than try to fight his way through. At Hodeibia, on the edge of the "sacred territory" surrounding Mecca, he drew up a treaty with the chiefs of the Koreish. All hostilities were to cease forthwith, there was to be a truce for ten years, and, in the future, starting the next year, the Muslims were to be permitted to pay an annual visit to the shrine and make the customary sacrifices. It was not all that the Prophet had hoped for, but, on his return to Medina, he made the most of the enforced delay by enlisting under his banner thousands of the Bedouin tribesmen in readiness for the next trial of strength.

The year soon passed, and then the Prophet set out once more for Mecca. This time there was no hitch. The gates were opened to him, and, surrounded by the rejoicing companions of his exile, he approached the Holy House, touched the Sacred Stone with his staff, and made the customary seven circuits, followed by the sacrifices and other time-honored rituals of the pilgrimage.

The agreement allowed for a stay in the holy city of only three days, and the Prophet, who had just added a new wife to his harem, would have liked to stay on a bit longer for the marriage feast. But the rulers of the city were adamant, and he had to leave. He had made excellent use of his time, however. The people had been edified by his show of devotion. The rulers of the Kaaba had been gratified by his assurance that, when he succeeded in his ambition of becoming the master of Mecca, the pilgrimages would continue as before,

although the idols must be destroyed. The military chiefs had
been impressed by his display of strength, and he had had
some highly satisfactory interviews with some of the most
important men. Among these was the valiant Khalid, who had
turned the tables on him at Uhud; he was sick of the present
regime, he assured the Prophet, and would be quite ready to
join him when the time was ripe.

4

The Lord of Arabia

Mohammed did not have long to wait. The treaty of Hodeibia was not a year old when the chiefs of the Koreish in Mecca were foolish enough to break the truce by attacking a tribe that had placed itself under the Prophet's protection. Mohammed struck at once. At the head of an army of 10,000 men, he set out for Mecca, and the news of his approach put the city in a panic. There was no attempt at negotiation. Mohammed summoned the rulers of Mecca to his camp outside the walls and dictated his terms.

Abu Sofyan, the chief of the Koreish, appeared humbly before him. "Are you ready to acknowledge at last," demanded the Prophet sternly, "that there is no god but Allah, and Mohammed is Allah's Apostle?"

The old man hesitated, whereupon (so the story goes)

Abbas (or it may have been Umar) flourished his sword
threateningly over his head. The chief made the required
submission, and the city's keys were handed over. There was
very little resistance; and what little there was, was soon put
down without any difficulty by Khalid, who had carried out
his promise to join Mohammed.

And now the great moment of the Prophet's life had come.
Mounted on his camel—the same camel (her name is given as
al-Kaswa) that had carried him away from the place eight
years before—Mohammed made his triumphal entry. Surrounded by excited crowds, he rode slowly through the
streets, until he came to the Kaaba, where he reverently
touched the Black Stone and made the seven prescribed
circuits. The key of the shrine was handed up to him, and
he returned it graciously to its hereditary custodian and confirmed him and his colleagues in their offices. Then he got
down from his camel and entered the holy place. With a
fierce gesture of hatred and contempt, he indicated the idols—
they are said to have numbered 360—that cluttered the shrine,
and bade that they be overthrown and destroyed. At his word,
men rushed forward and tore them from their stands and
niches, and, as they were smashed into dust beneath his feet,
the Prophet proclaimed the majesty of all-conquering Allah.

In the hour of triumph, he showed himself generous. Only
three or four of his most irreconcilable foes were ordered to
be executed. For all others, an amnesty was proclaimed. All
who made the profession of faith in Islam were assured of
their lives and the peaceable enjoyment of their possessions.
The Prophet's clemency was statesmanlike. Within a few
weeks, old animosities had been buried and forgotten, and a
Meccan regiment was fighting in the Muslim army against a
common foe.

This time, the enemy was a group of tribes called the Hawaizim, with whom were associated the Prophet's old opponents, the people of Taif. The battle occurred at a place called Hunain; the Muslims numbered 12,000 men and the confederates over 20,000. At the height of the engagement, Mohammed was surrounded by foes; several of his body-guards were slain, and he was preparing to die gloriously, when Abbas brought up reinforcements and turned the tide. The tribesmen fled in disorder, and Mohammed marched at once on Taif.

The town was well-defended, however, and, although Mohammed's men had battering-rams, they were unable to breach the walls. After twenty days, the retreat was sounded, and the Muslims had to console themselves with the booty gathered from their forays on the surrounding lands—but this was sufficient, we are told, to allow every man four camels and the leaders forty or fifty apiece. Before long the men of Taif thought it advisable to come to terms with Mohammed before he renewed the seige, and their deputies made a humble approach to him in his quarters.

"Grant us, O Apostle of Allah," they are reported to have said, "a truce of three years with the toleration of our ancient worship."

"What," the Prophet rejoined indignantly, "you dare to ask me to tolerate idolatry! Not a month, not a day, not an hour!"

"At least," begged the envoys, "excuse us from the obligation of prayer."

Again they met with a blunt refusal. "Without prayer," the Prophet told them, "religion is no use at all, " and the men from Taif were compelled to submit. They were left in possession of their lands, but they had to accept Islam and pay tribute; and it was with heavy hearts that they watched Mohammed's soldiers throwing down and trampling upon the beloved image of their goddess Allat.

After this, most of the Arabian tribes rushed to ally themselves with Mohammed and acknowledge his supremacy. To reach far-distant tribes, the Prophet had to extend the sphere of his military operations, and, in the last year of his life, he led an army of 30,000 men—the gest army he ever commanded—against a number of tribes in the north, which up to then had been tributary to the East Roman emperor. The enemy refused to give battle; it was the hottest season of the year, and men and camels suffered horribly from thirst. When his men grumbled, Mohammed turned on them fiercely. "Hell is much hotter!" he bade them remember. At Tabuk, on the borders of Syria, they turned back, but Mohammed had "shown the flag" and, within a few years, armies he had inspired were sweeping ahead in an avalanche of conquest.

In the spring of 632, Mohammed paid what was to prove his last visit to Mecca. In the history books it is referred to as the "Farewell Pilgrimage," and it was a purely Muslim gathering, for the Prophet announced that he had recently received a revelation from Allah prohibiting all non-Muslims from drawing near the Kaaba at the time of the annual pilgrimage. This injunction, it may be noted, has been strictly enforced, and it is estimated that no more than fifteen Christian-born Europeans have up to now succeeded in visiting the two holy cities of Mecca and Medina as pilgrims and lived to tell the tale.

At the height of the celebration, the Prophet preached a sermon whose words have echoed down the ages. According to the traditional account, these are some of the things he said.

"You people, listen to my words, for I do not know that

after this year I will ever be here among you again. Your lives and property are sacred and inviolable amongst one another until the end of time.

"Allah has ordained that every man shall receive the share of his inheritance. The child belongs to the parent. The violator of wedlock shall be stoned. Men have rights over their wives, and wives have rights demandable from their husbands. If your wives violate their conjugal faith or commit any act

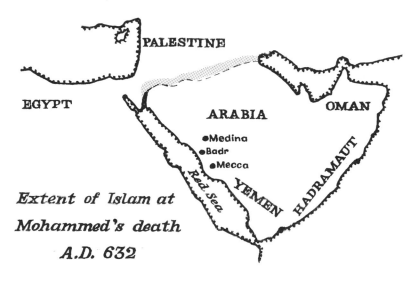

Extent of Islam at Mohammed's death A.D. 632

of open impropriety, you may shut them up in separate apartments and beat them with stripes, but not severely. If they refrain from such things, clothe them and feed them suitably. Treat the women well who are with you as prisoners and captives. Your slaves also: Feed them with the same food as you eat yourselves, and clothe them with the same clothes. And if they commit a fault that you cannot bring yourself to forgive, then sell them, for they also are the servants of Allah, and are not to be tormented."

There is nothing very revolutionary in these commandments, nor may they be considered as particularly enlightened and humane. But now follows a passage that is the title deed of the Brotherhood of Islam.

"O ye men, hearken unto my words, and take them to your heart! Know that every Muslim is a brother of every other Muslim, and that you are now one brotherhood. It is not lawful, therefore, for anyone among you to appropriate for himself anything that belongs to his brother, unless that brother gives it to him willingly."

Thus, by one stroke, the bond of tribal kinship that had bound together the Arabs, and only the Arabs, was replaced by a new bond—that of a common sharing of Islam. Within that brotherhood, all are equal in the sight of Allah.

When the Prophet returned to Medina from the pilgrimage, it was plain that he was sick, and it was rumored that he was suffering from some poison that had been given him by a hostile Jewess some years before. For fourteen days, he got steadily worse, and it was in the realization that his end was near that he mounted the pulpit in the mosque for the last time.

"Is there any Muslim here," he demanded of the assembled crowd, "whose reputation I have attacked? Then let him proclaim *my* faults in the face of the congregation. Have I despoiled anyone here of his goods? Do I owe any man anything? If so, the little that I have will be used to satisfy the principal and the interest of the debt."

A voice from the crowd asserted that the Prophet owed him a few pieces of silver. Mohammed paid the sum demanded, and publicly thanked his creditor for telling him of it rather than waiting until the Day of Judgment. Then, when he returned to his house, he enfranchised his slaves—seventeen men and eleven women—gave directions for his funeral, and solemnly blessed his weeping friends. Suddenly, he called for his scribe, and started dictating further passages for the book that was to become the Koran. His mind wandered back to his early days. Once again he saw Gabriel, and was confirmed in his faith.

Once he had declared that Allah had given him, as a mark of very special favor, the right to choose the date of his death. Now he said the word: He was ready, and eager, to depart. In the room of Ayesha, his favorite wife, he lay on the ground on a carpet, with his head in her lap. "Oh Allah, pardon my sins . . . ," the dying man was heard to murmur, "I come . . . among the glorious associates on High!" Then he was dead. The day was Monday, June 8, 632.

At first, some of those standing round refused to believe it. "Our Prophet can't be dead," they exclaimed hysterically, "he's only sleeping!" Umar threatened to cut off the head of any man who asserted that the Prophet was no more. Then Abu Bakr spoke. "Do you worship Mohammed," he demanded quietly, "or Mohammed's God? *He* lives forever, but the Prophet was a man like ourselves and has paid the price of mortality." Umar lowered his sword, and, to the solemn wailing of a great multitude, the Apostle of Allah was laid to rest in the place where he had died.

5

The Apostle
of Allah

The Prophet was dead, but the influence of that astonishing man was only beginning. He, an unlettered man, left behind him a book, or rather the raw material for a book, which has changed the lives of millions. This is the Koran, and we shall learn something about it in the next chapter. But here let us take a closer look at Mohammed. What sort of man was he?

We know what he looked like. Although he was only of medium height, he was not the sort of man who could get lost easily in a crowd. He had a commanding presence. He was sturdily built, with broad shoulders, long arms, and a large head with a high and broad forehead. He had jet-black hair as a young man, and, when it turned gray, he still wore it long. His beard was full and bushy. He had deep black piercing eyes, a hooked nose, and a mouth that was on the large side. The nicest thing about him was his smile.

If we had met him one day walking along the street, we would have had difficulty keeping up with him, for he walked fast just as he talked fast. His head and body were thrust forward, as if he were rushing uphill; to use one of today's expressions, he looked as if he were hurrying to catch a train.

One of the things that people remembered about him was that in shaking hands he was never the first to withdraw his own, "nor was he the first to break off a conversation with a stranger, nor turn away his ear." He was a companionable man. He treated the most insignificant persons with kindly consideration, and yet could hold his own with the great ones of the world. He sympathized with people's little joys and griefs. Women were strongly attracted to him, and he was particularly good with children.

But, although he was gentle in his manner, kind and courteous, he was also capable of fierce anger. At such times, a vein in his forehead swelled up "black like a horseshoe." Those who knew him came to recognize it as a sort of danger signal.

In his personal life, he lived simply. When he had become ruler of Medina, a king in all but name, he still lived very much as he had done when he was Khadija's business manager. He despised the pomp of royalty. Foreigners who had learned to dread his name heard with amazement that he was in the habit of getting up early in the morning and lighting the fire in his modest home, that he swept the floor and carried away the rubbish, that he milked the ewes, that he mended his own shoes and patched with his own hands the cloak that was his usual garb. For weeks on end, it was reported, he would go without a fire in his room. He never drank wine, but he liked a cup of milk and generally made do with water. He liked honey with his barley bread, and occasionally as a special treat had a loaf made of wheat flour. He usually dined off a handful of dates. There was one little luxury that he allowed himself—a touch of perfume.

One thing more may be noted about him: his kindness to animals. In this he was exceptional. There is a story told of him that once, when he was marching along with his troops, they came across a dog with her puppies lying right in their line of march. Some rough fellow was about to kick them out of the way, but Mohammed stopped him. They were not to be disturbed, he ordered sternly; and to make sure that his order was obeyed, he placed a sentry on guard beside the dog until all the men had gone past.

We are not told that Mohammed ever kept a dog, but he was certainly very fond of cats. He had a favorite cat that accompanied him wherever he went, and he took pains to see that she was comfortable. When, years ago, a home for cats was opened in Damascus, the reason given was that the Prophet had been so attached to them. Once (so the story ran) when he had visited the city, he brought his cat, which slept in the sleeve of his garment, and, one day, rather than disturb his little friend, he cut off the sleeve so that she might sleep on in peace.

As a good Arab, he knew all there was to know about camels. Once, a woman who had only just managed to escape from some raiders by the speed of her camel told him that she had vowed to sacrifice the camel to Allah if she got away safely. "That's a poor reward," commented the Prophet with a smile. "Allah saved you by her, and then you want to kill her! Leave the poor beast alone, and go home with Allah's blessing!"

Children, as was mentioned just now, got on well with him. He had many friends among them, and he had no difficulty in entering into the spirit of their childish games. It must have been a great grief to him when his own two boys died in infancy; but he had his daughters, and mention is made of a favorite granddaughter, called Umamah, whom he was wont to carry on his shoulders to the public prayers. One of his wives, his favorite, Ayesha, was only a little girl of eight when he married her; she was still playing with her dolls and she brought them with her to her new home. Toward the end of his life, he had a son by Mary, the Egyptian slave girl, but, after eighteen months, little Ibrahim died, and the Prophet grieved deeply as he smoothed the earth over the little grave with his hands. "This doesn't help or harm the dead," he said, "but it eases the afflicted heart, it is a comfort to the living. . . ."

What a good person he must have been—such a kind man, who had such a way with children and a soft spot in his heart for animals, who disliked "showing off." And yet it has been said, and it is probably true, that Mohammed has been the most maligned of all the world's great men. There is hardly anything that has been thought too bad to say about him—by non-Muslims, that is.

The reason for this lies, of course, in his religion. Since it came into the world through his preaching, Islam has been regarded, and rightly regarded, as Christianity's most dangerous enemy. To the Europe of the Middle Ages, "Mahound" (as the Prophet was opprobriously called) was the close ally of the Prince of Darkness, if he were not the Devil himself; how otherwise might the success of the Muslim armies be accounted for! That attitude has remained through all the centuries that have since passed, and even today it is unusual to find a sympathetic account of the Prophet and his work.

Beyond any doubt, there were some very grave defects in Mohammed's character. He was sometimes quite unscrupulous, as when he sanctioned the attack on the Meccan caravan during a month of truce. He was cruel sometimes, as when he sanctioned the massacre of the Jews at Koraiza. There is reason to believe that on more than one occasion he resorted to assassination to rid himself of particularly obnoxious critics. He was relentless in war, destroying crops and houses, slaughtering the men, and selling the women and children into slavery. All this and more must be laid to his account.

But we should be on our guard against judging him by the standards of the most enlightened opinion of the present instead of by those of his own country and period. It is to be noted that his character had few critics in his own generation and circle, even among those who had no reason to fear his ill will. And when criticisms *were* voiced, it was not so much on the ground that his actions were immoral as that they were politically dangerous—for instance, the attack on the caravan mentioned above. This did not strike his contemporaries as wicked, but they *did* feel that he went too far in challenging the pagan gods and the superstitious fears of the people. Similarly, the massacre of the Jews amazed them, because of the huge number of blood-feuds that might be created by the slaughter. When Mohammed triumphed, their doubts were dispelled and their belief in him as a prophet was greatly strengthened.

Then there is the question of his "lustfulness," his "sensuality." While Khadija was alive, he was the faithful husband of one wife, but when she died he "fell into polygamous ways." This is true enough; about a score of women are said to have become his wives, and thirteen of them are remembered by name. At his death, there were nine wives in his harem, who were henceforth styled "mothers of the Believers" and forbidden to marry again. He declared as the will of Allah that Muslims should be allowed to have four wives at a time, and no more than four although the number of concubines was left unlimited. But he maintained that he had been granted special privileges by Allah "above the rest of the true believers."

All this is true, but Mohammed did not institute or "invent" polygamy: it was something that had existed since time immemorial in Arabia as in other Eastern lands, and has continued up to the present. And while polygamy as an institution tends toward female subordination to the male, there is also a good deal to be said for it in societies in which there is nothing in the nature of social security, no old-age and widows' pensions, no public assistance. Furthermore, there is good reason to believe that quite a number of the Prophet's marriages were political: There was no surer means of securing the assistance or ensuring the loyalty of the father than by marrying his daughter. There is also reason to believe that the number of his wives has been exaggerated, since it came to be considered among the Arabian tribes that it was a great honor to have had an ancestress who was included in his harem.

Beyond any question, Mohammed was fond of women, and women were deeply attracted to him. But, here again, it should be noted that his contemporaries, his friends and associates, and even his enemies found nothing in this that was strange or worthy of condemnation. Like most Arabs, the Prophet believed that marriage was a Divine institution and that every man should be married, and, so far as possible, every woman likewise. He despised the Christian hermits, monks, and nuns who boasted of their celibacy. In his opinion, it was the duty of every true believer to marry and have a family and bring up the children in the fear and love of Allah.

Now we come to the last of the charges laid against Mohammed. He was an imposter, it is alleged; he was thoroughly insincere, he did not really believe that he was God's chosen prophet, he "invented" Islam as a means of satisfying his ambition for power and domination, not to mention the gratification of his sensual lusts. This is the sort of charge that was brought against Mohammed in generations gone by, and notwithstanding Thomas Carlyle's warm protests against it in his *Heroes and Hero Worship*—"a false man found a religion? Why, a false man cannot build a brick house!"—it is still sometimes heard. But it is not valid.

Born into genteel poverty, Mohammed made an advantageous marriage, after which he need never have done another day's work unless he wanted to. He could have idled away his life in the coffee shops and sunk himself in the selfish pleasures of the wealthy. Instead of this, he busied himself with his wife's affairs and played his full part in the government of the town. And then he became religious. What had he to gain by his midnight wanderings in the desert, his preachings against the established religion, his antagonizing of the most important men of his tribe and family? He was no youngster thirsting for fame and adventure but a middle-aged man of forty when the "call" came to him. He might have been excused for preferring a quiet life in the comfort of his home, instead of which he chose persecution and hostility, hardship and danger, the loss of home and friends and reputation. He went out almost alone from among his own people and sought help and understanding from strangers. He might have kept quiet. But, in fact, he shouted out his message, what he believed to be true, the truest of truths, and eventually, at his call, the Arabs awoke from their age-old slumbers and rode out of the desert to destroy empires and carve out new ones, to challenge ancient wrongs and superstitions, to build a new civilization in which millions of people would work out their destiny.

It was a colossal achievement, and no imposter could have done it, no schemer, no charlatan, but only a man who *believed* in the truth of what he preached. This is not the same as saying that what Mohammed believed to be true *is* true, or at least the whole truth, but non-Muslims can surely join with Muslims in paying a tribute to the Prophet's overwhelming sincerity.

6

The Koran

When Mohammed was living in Medina, there was a chest in the livingroom into which were popped, from time to time, scraps of parchment and leather, camels' shoulder blades, mutton bones, ribs of palm leaves, pieces of board, and other bits and pieces on which there was writing. This collection of oddments was the basis of the Koran, the book which is the holy scripture of the Muslims, their holiest book, their Bible.

Sometimes it is said that Mohammed was the author of the Koran. Nothing could be more offensive to Muslims, and they claim the statement could be made only by persons who are ignorant and prejudiced. To say that the Prophet wrote the Koran is, in Muslim ears, the most shocking blasphemy. According to the accepted Muslim belief, the Koran had no human author, but was written by Allah, God Himself. From the beginning of things, the original has rested on a vast table that is placed at the side of God's throne in Heaven, but a copy, in one volume on paper, bound in silk and adorned with precious stones, was carried down from Heaven by the Angel Gabriel and shown to Mohammed once a year. From this volume, Gabriel dictated passages and chapters at different times, over the space of twenty-three years. Few of the chapters were delivered complete, but for the most part they were given piecemeal. What Gabriel told him, the Prophet repeated to his secretaries, who were in waiting to take down what fell from his lips. They had no neatly ruled notebooks, but had to make do with the first thing that came to hand. In these circumstances, it is hardly surprising that the contents sometimes seem a bit muddled. But there can be no complaints about the language; it is Arabic of the purest kind.

The word "Koran" comes from the Arabic *quran*, meaning "reading," "lecture," or "recitation" or perhaps "that which ought to be read." Sometimes it is called *al kitab*, "the book," to emphasize its superiority over every other book. It is about three-quarters the length of the New Testament in Arabic. According to one Muslim statistician, who took the trouble of counting, it has 77,639 words, but another makes the count 77,934. The number of verses is given as 6,236. Someone has even counted the letters, making the total 323,015, and someone else has made it 323,621.

Like the Bible, the Koran is divided into chapters. The technical name for a chapter is *sura;* there are 114 suras, which are arranged roughly in order of length, the longest ones being put first. If the suras were arranged chronologically, the order would have to be reversed, for the longer suras are mainly those dating from the period when Mohammed was established in Medina, while the shorter ones belong to the Meccan period, when he was still the persecuted prophet.

A page from a richly illuminated Koran, inscribed in gold, that was made for the Great Chamberlain al-Rubri in A.D. 1304–5.

The suras belonging to this time of struggle are short, pithy, fiery, and impassioned in style. The Medinese suras are much longer and wordy, suggesting that the Prophet was not so pressed for time as in his earlier days, but it should be remarked that their subjects are mainly matters of doctrine and laws and regulations concerning such important things as marriage and divorce, crimes, inheritance, etc., which cannot be dealt with briefly.

But there is one principal exception to the rule just noted: The opening chapter of the Koran is one of the shortest. It contains only a half-dozen lines, and it is a prayer that is repeated by faithful Muslims about twenty times each day. It is the Muslim counterpart of the Christian Lord's Prayer. It is called the *Fatihah*, and here it is, as translated by J. M. Rodwell:

> Praise be to God, Lord of the worlds!
> The compassionate, the merciful!
> King on the day of judgment!
> Thee only do we worship, and to Thee do we cry for help.
> Guide Thou us on the right path,
> The path of those to whom Thou art gracious,
> Not of those with whom Thou art angered, nor of those who
>   go astray.

Every sura except the ninth begins with the words, "In the Name of the Most Merciful God," or, as some modern translators put it, "In the Name of God (or Allah), the Compassionate, the Merciful." The Arabic for "In the Name of God" is *bismillah*, which word is frequently encountered in descriptions of Muslim life. Each sura has a heading, such as "The Cow" or "Women" or "The Bee," and some of the chapters bear mysterious numbers, which scholars do not fully understand. The derivation of the word "sura" is also not known for sure, but most probably it referred originally to a row or order, like a layer of bricks in a wall, or a rank of soldiers on the parade ground.

In all but the opening verses and a very few other passages, the book is written in the first person. It is Allah, God Himself, who is speaking, and from beginning to end it is regarded by Muslims as the infallible Word of God. For hundreds of years, they were firmly persuaded that it contained within its covers everything that was worth knowing, and to this day it has remained the basis of law for the Muslim peoples, the foundation of their legal, judicial, and political systems, and a completely reliable and authoritative guide in every aspect of their daily lives.

As was already mentioned, it is written in the purest Arabic, the language that is used today by some 50 million people as the medium of daily expression, and whose alphabet is, next to the Latin, the most widely used in the world. Unlike Latin, Arabic has not developed into a number of different languages such as French, Italian, and Spanish, but (because the Koran was composed in Arabic) it remains the classical language of the Muslim peoples almost everywhere. Moroccans, Iraqis, Egyptians, Arabs, and Syrians, while speaking rather different dialects so that they might have difficulty in understanding one another, all understand the written language—again because it is that of the Koran.

In the Middle Ages, Arabic was the language of learning and culture and progressive thought throughout the civilized world, and the languages of Western Europe still bear the impress of its influence. In our own English speech, there are numerous Arabic words, for instance, admiral, alcohol, algebra, almanac, apricot, caravan, coffee, cotton, crimson, giraffe, jasmine, lemon, mattress, shrub, sugar, sultan, and zero.

The Koran is the textbook from which every Muslim learns Arabic, and it is the basis of education, whether in such great universities as al-Azhar at Cairo—the largest Muslim university in the world—or in the village schools where, as for centuries past, the schoolmaster sits on the floor surrounded by his pupils, who chant its verses in a kind of sing-song until they know most of it by heart. This is the way it should be learned, for (we are assured) it sounds much better when it is recited than when it is read in silence. Only then can its rhyme and cadence be properly appreciated.

Until the Koran was composed, there was no important prose work in the Arabic language, nothing much more than martial lays and love songs. It was the first, and has remained ever since the model, prose work in the language. Since no official translation of the book was made until recent times, what is called Koranic Arabic served as a common language and a bond of brotherhood between Muslims everywhere.

Naturally enough, Muslims hold the book in the greatest reverence and treat it with the utmost respect. When it is being read aloud, there must be no smoking or drinking, no conversation. The sacred volume is kept on a high shelf, and no other book, or anything else, must be placed on top of it. It is frequently dusted and is kept scrupulously clean. Muslims wash their hands before touching it, are most careful not to drop it, and never hold it below their waists. They think it improper that it should be even touched by a non-Muslim. It is a talisman against sickness and disaster. Some pious Muslims never go out without a copy in their pockets, so that they can improve their time by reading a page or two when waiting for a train or traveling. When a visitor enters a sickroom, he or she quotes appropriate verses from the Koran, and often the book is read right through by the watchers over a corpse. When Muslims quote from it, they usually say, "Allah, Whose Name be exalted, hath said, in the Excellent Book."

Muslims take their most solemn oaths on the Koran, and

the superstitious ones among them dip into its pages for good omens. Those who can afford it have their copies bound in splendid covers adorned with jewels. Soldiers take the Koran into battle with them, and verses from the holy book have been inscribed on their banners. In the mosques or places of Muslim worship, no statues or pictures are allowed, but on the walls are painted, in the beautiful flowing Arabic script, verses from the Koran.

What does the Koran contain? The best way to learn the answer is of course to read it, and that is what everybody should do, or at least try to do. For it must be admitted that it is not an easy book to get through. It is not nearly as interesting as the Bible. But it should be remembered that the Bible is not one book, as the Koran is, but a whole library of books, composed over a period of more than a thousand years. Thomas Carlyle confessed that the Koran was "as toilsome reading as I ever undertook. A wearisome confused jumble . . . . Nothing but a sense of duty could carry any European through the Koran." (But Carlyle also wrote, in the very next paragraph, that "the primary character of the Koran is its genuineness.")

The translation that he found so toilsome was the 1734 one by George Sale, an English lawyer, and it cannot really be as hard going as Carlyle claimed, or it would not have passed through so many editions right up to our own time. Sale's "Preliminary Discourse" is particularly valuable, and indeed his translation opened a new chapter in the study of Islam and its Prophet. There have been a number of other versions: the one by the Rev. J. M. Rodwell in 1861 that is published in "Everyman's Library"; the one by the Cambridge scholar E. H. Palmer (1880) that was used for the "World's Classics" edition; Marmaduke Pickthall's *The Meaning of the Glorious*

Koran (1930), the first English translation of the Koran by an English Muslim; Richard Bell's (1937); Professor A. J. Arberry's *The Koran Interpreted* (1955); and N. J. Dawood's translation in the "Penguin Classics" that appeared in 1956, which is an attempt at "an intelligible version of the Koran in contemporary English." Whichever translation is used, it will be found that the Koran contains many passages that are boring. But even so, it is surely worth the effort to read, and try to understand, the book that to hundreds of millions of our fellow men is the Word of God and the Rule of Life.

In the main, the Koran is concerned with the All-wise, All-good, All-loving, and All-powerful God whom the Muslims know as Allah. Chapter after chapter contains descriptions of His goodness and mercy, while other chapters emphasize His hatred of sin and His sternness in judgment and readiness to punish. Idolatry, the worship of images, is fiercely condemned. The joys of Heaven are pictured in glowing phrases, which are equaled in vivid intensity by the pictures of the pains of Hell. Human history is seen as a great drama which will be wound up and terminated at the Day of Judgment when "the trumpet shall sound a single blast, the earth shall be moved from its place, and the mountains also, and shall be dashed to pieces at a single stroke, and the heavens shall cleave in sunder and fall to pieces. . . . On that day shall you all be presented before the Judgment Seat of Allah, and none of your secret actions shall be hid."

There are many references to the "prophets" of God in days gone by. We meet many of the famous characters of the Old Testament and two or three of those who appear in the New Testament. Time and again, some of the best known of the Bible stories are told in different words, and sometimes with considerable differences, due (it has been suggested) to the Prophet's having obtained his knowledge of the Bible from the lips of men and not from the books themselves.

Then there are passages of moral guidance, directions on what to do and what not to do in certain circumstances, answers to special questions, laws, and rules of living.

What the Koran teaches about Islam and its practical requirements will be described in the next section, but we should first look at the way in which the holy book came into existence and has been preserved and handed down.

As we have already learned, the suras, or parts of suras, were written down by scribes or secretaries as the words fell from the Prophet's lips, either when he was still in a trance or sunk in vision or when he had returned to full consciousness. Not everything was written down, it seems; quite a number of the suras were first put into writing after his death. Only when he was dead and there could be no more revelations, was the importance of putting on record what he had said properly realized. There was nothing, of course, in the Prophet's own handwriting.

In the year following Mohammed's death, his successor (or caliph, from the Arabic *khalifa*) in the leadership of the Muslim realm, Abu Bakr, commissioned a young man of twenty-two, one Zayd ibn-Thabit, of Medina, who had been the Prophet's secretary, to collect the scattered portions of the "revelations" and see if he could put them in some sort of order. So Zayd went to the chest which was still standing in a corner of the Prophet's house and took out the stones, leather scraps, bones, palm ribs, etc., and wrote out a fair copy of what was inscribed on them. He also included a lot more material that he gathered from the "breasts of men"—that is, what the Prophet's associates remembered of what they had heard him say. Abu Bakr received the copy, and passed it on to his successor, Umar. When Umar died, he left it to his daughter Hafsa, who was one of Mohammed's widows.

Then, about 650—nearly twenty years after Mohammed's death—Zayd and three prominent members of the Koreish were entrusted with the job of making a fresh version. So they collected as many copies of the previous version as they could find; these were carefully compared, and from them a fresh version was prepared, which it was decided should be regarded henceforth as canonical, or altogether standard and authoritative. To prevent any future disputes, the editors burned all other copies.

Three fair copies were made of the new version, and one was sent to each of the three military camps that had now been established as the capitals of the rapidly growing Muslim empire—Damascus, Basra, and Kufa—while the original copy was preserved in the mosque at Medina. In matters of spelling and other small points, the copies differed somewhat, but these variations nowhere affected the sense. All later manuscripts of the Koran have derived from these four copies. There is no reason to doubt that in the Koran we have, in the main, the actual words that Mohammed used 1,300 years ago when he uttered his pronouncements as the messenger of the Most High God.

It has been stated that the Koran is the most widely read and quoted book in the world, more so than even the Bible. This may well be true, since passages from the holy book enter into the daily ritual of every Muslim. The first chapter, the Fatihah, is recited several times at each of the five daily prayers.

The Arabic text is the only official one, with the exception of one in Turkish, but a number of interlinear translations exist in Persian, Bengali, Urdu, Javanese, Chinese, and other languages used by great numbers of Muslims. In all, the Koran has been translated into about forty languages. The first translation was into Latin in about 1143; it was done by an English scholar named Robertus Retenensis for Peter the Venerable, abbot of the great abbey of Cluny, in France. The first printed edition in Arabic was produced at Venice in 1485.

When, from time to time, Mohammed was challenged to work miracles such as other prophets were reported to have done, in evidence of his claims to the possession of apostolic powers, he always indignantly refused. He was no miracle-worker, he exclaimed. But if his critics really wanted to see a miracle, they hadn't far to look. The Koran was surely the greatest miracle that could be performed!

To those people who said that "It is Mohammed's own invention: he has forged it," he rejoined, "Compose just one chapter like it! Call on your false gods to help you, if what you say is true!" And when they stood silent, he went on, "This Koran couldn't possibly have been composed by anyone but Allah. It confirms everything that has been revealed before now, and fully explains the Scriptures. Yes, indeed, it is Allah's work."

7

Islam: What a Muslim Believes

Although it is often incorrectly called Mohammedanism, the proper name for the religion that the Prophet preached is *Islam*. This is the name that he himself chose, and it means "submission" or "surrender" of oneself to God. Those who profess Islam are known as Muslims (or Moslems)—a word that comes from the same Arabic root and means "those who have surrendered themselves to God," or "believers," as opposed to those who have rejected the faith. A variation sometimes met with is Musulman; this is the Persian form of the word.

"Muslim" or "Moslem" is preferred by believers in Islam themselves. "Mohammedan" is convenient, but they feel that it may give a wrong impression. Christians worship Christ, and hence "Christian" is quite the proper word to describe them. But Muslims *do not* worship Mohammed, although they hold most firmly that he was the greatest of the line of prophets or messengers sent into this world by God or Allah. When they speak of him, they usually add after his name, "On whom be peace and the blessings of God!"

To be a Muslim means that a man *believes* certain things and *does* certain things. To take the beliefs, or *iman*, first, the creed or statement of faith in Islam is short and simple. It is called the *Shahada*, and in translation it runs: "There is no god but God (Allah), and Mohammed is the Apostle (or Prophet, or Messenger) of God."

Every page of the Koran bears witness to Mohammed's belief in God—or Allah, to use the Muslim form. *Allah* is a shortened form of *al-ilah*, "the god," and, as we have seen, it was in use among the Arabs long before Mohammed's time. But it was he who gave it its supreme importance. The Allah of the pagan Arabs was only the chief god among numerous other divinities; the Allah preached by Mohammed is the One and Only God. As a very famous passage in the Koran—the so-called Throne verse in Sura 2—puts it:

> Allah! There is no God but He, the Living, the Eternal One!
> He neither slumbers nor sleeps.
> Everything in Heaven and in earth belongs to Him.
> Who shall intercede with Him without His permission?
> He knows all that is past and all that is to come.
> Men understand nothing of what He knows unless He wills.
> Over Heaven and earth extends His Throne,
> Their preservation is not the slightest trouble to Him,
> The Most-high, the All-glorious One.

To Mohammed, Allah was the supreme reality, the most *real* thing in all the world; in fact, He is the *only* reality. "Don't you dare to call on any other god than Allah," he commanded his followers; "serve none besides Him. There is no other god but Allah. All things must perish except Himself. He is the judge, His the judgment. To Him we shall all return."

"Allah is mighty and wise," declared the Prophet in another passage. "He gives life and He puts to death. He is the first and the last, the seen and the hidden. He is with you wherever you may be. God sees everything that we do. He knows every man's innermost thoughts. Not a leaf falls, but He knows it. He sends his guardian angels to watch over us, and to bear away our souls when the time comes for us to die."

It is Allah who creates man out of a grain of dust. He distinguishes man from woman. Not a woman conceives and bears a child without His knowing. No man grows old or has his life cut short unless it is His will. "All this is easy to Allah."

We can imagine the Prophet, standing in the market place in Mecca or seated amongst his small congregation in a friend's house, reminding his hearers of the innumerable good things that God has showered upon His creation. His sermon is given in a chapter that is called, rather quaintly, "The Bee" (because in it bees are praised for their ingenuity). "He created you all, each man of you, from a little germ, and yet you have the audacity to challenge His judgments! He has given you horses and mules and donkeys. He sends down the rain from heaven, so that you may have water to drink, and water to nourish your cattle, and to make your corn grow, and your olives, palm trees, and grapes. Surely there is something here for thinking men to ponder! It is Allah who has given you dominion over the earth, and has made the sea subject to you, so that you can catch fish to eat and also have ornaments (such as pearls and coral) to deck yourself with. Think of the ships ploughing the waves in order that you may become rich through commerce! It is Allah who has provided roads and rivers and other landmarks, so that you won't lose your way. The stars, also, in the sky. Allah has furnished you with houses to live in, and tents made from skins, that may be taken down and carted about so easily. He has provided trees to shade you from the sun, and caves as places of refuge in the desert. He has given you clothes to protect you from the heat, and coats of armor to protect you when you go to the wars. He has given you good things to eat and drink. He has given you wives, and children, and grandchildren. After all this, how can you possibly deny that God is good? How can you persist in bowing down in worship to idols made of wood and stone, saying that *they* are your gods?"

Mohammed's faith in Allah is summed up in the shortest chapter in the Koran, Sura 112: "Say, God is One, the eternal God! He begetteth not, neither is He begotten. And there is not any one like unto Him."

Here in two lines we have expressed in its simplest form the really fundamental belief of Islam, the absolute Oneness or Unity of God. Its acceptance involves the complete and utter repudiation of all the gods and goddesses of the pagan pantheons. It also involves the rejection of the fundamental doctrine of Christianity—the divinity of Jesus Christ.

In the Koran, Jesus is often referred to, and never without deep respect. He is styled "Jesus, the son of Mary," and the Virgin Birth is affirmed. He is acknowledged to have worked miracles, and to have been one of the noble line of God's prophets. So highly is he thought of, indeed, that it is indignantly denied that he was crucified; this would have been too great an indignity for so honorable a prophet to have undergone, and another died on the Cross in his place. It is even held that, at some time before the general resurrection of the dead, Jesus will return to earth and rule in Jerusalem for forty years, after which time he will die and be buried beside the Prophet in the mosque at Medina, where a vacant tomb is said to be kept in readiness. But Muslims deny that Jesus is God, and they are particularly indignant with the phrase "God's Son" that is applied to him. "Allah has no consort," they declare; "how then could He have a son?"

Besides the *Shahada*, there is a short passage in the Koran that is sometimes taken as being the nearest approach in Islam to the Apostles' Creed of Christianity. It is contained in Sura 4 and runs as follows: "O true believers, believe in God and His Apostle, and the scripture which He hath caused to descend unto His Apostle, and the scriptures which He hath formerly sent down. And whosoever does not believe in God, and His angels, and His scriptures, and His Apostles, and the Last Day, he surely has strayed a very long way from the truth."

From this, it will be clear that Mohammed taught that Islam was a continuation of the religions that had gone before. He did not look upon himself as the founder of a new religion, but as one who had been commissioned by Allah to restore the faith in all its original purity that Allah had revealed to Adam and Abraham and their successors in the line of "prophets."

Twenty-eight of these divinely inspired men are mentioned by name in the Koran, and, of these, eighteen are Old Testament characters and three are drawn from the New Testament (Zacharias, his son John the Baptist, and Jesus Christ). The last of the line of prophets is Mohammed, who is considered to have been Allah's Apostle not to one race and country only but to all mankind. In Muslim estimation, Mohammed is the last and greatest, the "Seal" of the prophetic line.

"The scripture (or book) which Allah caused to descend" is the Koran, and the other scriptures or books are those of the Jews and Christians. It is held that there were 104 God-given books, but all save four of these have long since perished and vanished away. The four survivors are the Jewish Torah, which consists of the Pentateuch or "Books of Moses" in the Old Testament; the Psalms of King David in the same volume; the Gospel of Jesus contained in the New Testament; and last, and the most authoritative, the Koran. All are true, but the Koran contains the whole and final truth.

The angels are often mentioned in the Koran. They are represented as God's messengers, always in readiness to do His bidding. They worship Him continually. They hold up His throne, descend to earth from time to time with His decrees, keep in a book a record of every man's actions, and receive men's souls when they die. Among the most important of the angelic host is Gabriel, who dictated the Koran to Mohammed. In addition to the good angels, there is supposed to be a class of supernatural beings, called jinn, who are mostly of an evil character.

Finally, we come to the doctrine of the Last Day. The Arabians of Mohammed's time were pagan idolaters, who had the haziest notions about the future life; most of them didn't believe there is any such thing. In the Koran, we are told the kinds of remarks they made when Mohammed preached the doctrine of the resurrection of the dead. "Does he threaten you that, after you are dead and have been turned to dust and bones, you will be brought forth alive from your grave? Away with such rubbish! We live, and we die, and that's the end of it. There's no life besides the present one. We won't be raised again, you may be very sure!"

The Prophet's warnings were dismissed as old wives' tales. But he persisted. "This present life," he maintained solemnly, "is nothing more than a toy, a plaything, a vain amusement. We may be very sure that what comes after will be very much better—for those who love Allah."

When a man dies and his body is laid in the grave, the Prophet explained, he is visited on the first night by two angels of very horrid appearance. Their names are Munkar and Nakir. They order the corpse to sit up, and proceed to examine him concerning his beliefs. "Who is your God? Who is your Prophet? What is your faith? Which is your book? Where is your kiblah?" (This last is the direction toward which one turns in prayer.)

Every Muslim knows what the answers should be, for the grim scene is referred to at funerals. As the body is laid in the grave, the imam, or officiating minister, addresses it in some such terms as, "O Son of Adam, when the two angels come to question you, answer them, "God, greatest in glory, is my only Lord; Mohammed, my Prophet; Islam, my faith; the Koran, my book; and the Holy House at Mecca, my kiblah."

If these are the answers, the two angels leave the dead man in peace; if otherwise, they beat him with iron hammers. Then follows what is called "the interval," during which the wicked are given a nasty foretaste of the punishments that will be their final lot, while the good souls stay somewhere near their graves. Mohammed (we are told) used to salute the spirits of the dead whenever he passed a graveyard: They could hear the friendly greetings just as well as the living, he declared. According to other Muslim teachings, however, the good souls rest with Adam in the lowest of the series of heavens, or they are sunk in the well Zem-zem beside the Kaaba, or they are inside the trumpet which will sound on the last day,

A devotee reads the Koran near the marble pulpit of the Jamma Masjid mosque in New Delhi.

or they dwell in the shape of white birds under the Throne of Allah.

So, in one way or another, the interval will be spent, and the great Day of Resurrection will draw near. Mohammed asked Gabriel when it would be, but the angel replied that he didn't know: Only Allah knew. But it would be preceded by a number of telltale signs; some small, such as the promotion of unworthy persons to positions of dignity, and the supplanting of the mistress in the home by the maidservant, and some big ones, including the sun's rising in the West, the appearance of a fearsome she-monster somewhere in the neighborhood of the Kaaba, and the return of Jesus to earth, to reign for forty years as already mentioned—years during which there will be a stop to hatred and malice, and lions and camels, bears and sheep will lie down together in perfect harmony.

Then a great trumpet blast will announce the great day of reckoning. The earth will be shaken and shattered, the heavens will melt, the sea will dry up. Another blast, and everything living will die. Yet another tremendous blast, and the bones of the dead will rush together, souls will be reunited with their bodies. All mankind will be resurrected in the same naked state as that in which they were born. (When Ayesha, Mohammed's young and favorite wife, heard this, she objected that surely it would be most improper for men and women to see each other in that state? Mohammed is said to have rejoined that they would be far too busy with much more weighty matters to be interested in anything improper. But some writers claim the Prophet's authority for the view that the dead will be raised wearing the same clothes that they had died in.)

Clothed or unclothed, the resurrected will be lined up on

the assembly ground, and put through a number of painful
and humiliating ordeals. At length, Allah will appear through
the clouds to act as Judge, and Mohammed will be given the
post of intercessor, making out the best possible case for his
believers. For the Judgment will be a sort of accounting. A
man will be asked (so Mohammed declared) how he spent
his time on earth. Did he look after his body properly, and
how did he develop his understanding? If he was wealthy,
how did he come by his riches, and in what way did he make
use of them? To these and other questions, everybody will
answer the best he can, and there will be no chance of getting
away with any false statement or silly excuse, for each man
will be given a book in which all his deeds are written down.
If it is a good record on the whole, he will be given the book
to hold in his right hand; if he is given it to hold in his left,
then that is a very bad sign indeed.

After this, the man's account will be weighed in a balance
held by Gabriel. If the pan containing the good deeds dips
down, he will be saved and pardoned; if the one holding the
bad deeds is the heavier, then he will be condemned.

When all the trials have been completed—how long that
will take is a matter in dispute (some think that it will all be
over in the time between two milkings of a she camel, whereas
others think that it may require thousands of years)—the
crowd will be divided into the saved and the condemned.
The former will be shepherded along the right-hand path that
leads to Paradise, and the latter urged along the one that leads
to the other place. But all have first to pass over the bridge
called al-Sirat, which is described as being finer than a hair
and sharper than a sword and beset on either side by thick
briers. Mohammed and his Muslims will go charging across
the bridge without any hesitation, and reach the other

side quite safely. But the others, the wicked, what with the narrowness and slipperiness of the path and the grasping prickles, may fall over the edge into the abyss of hell that lies gaping beneath.

Let us follow the righteous as they pour over al-Sirat. Hardly are they across, when they will be invited to refresh themselves at the "Pond of the Prophet," a huge reservoir of water kept supplied by pipes running from the rivers of Paradise; the water is described as being whiter than milk and sweeter-smelling than musk, and whoever drinks of it will never thirst again. Just outside the gates of Paradise are two fountains—in one, the pilgrims wash off every stain of travel, and, from the other, take a drink that purifies them of every ill. Now the gates fly open, a voice bids them welcome, and angels, two to each man, step forward and make presents of a beautiful robe and a ring of surpassing value. In addition to these angelic attendants, each person is allotted a number of handsome youths, whose business it is to run their errands and serve them in every capacity.

The delights of Heaven are recounted at length in several passages of the Koran. They are such as would be most calculated to appeal to the Arabian temperament. There are trees laden with fruit, there are silken garments, there are fine horses ready saddled and bridled, there are springs and fountains and rivers, flowing not only with water but with milk or wine or honey. Above all, there are the *houris*, the black-eyed girls of Paradise (the word comes, it may be noted, from the Arabic *huriya*, a black-eyed girl). "The companions of the right hand, how happy they shall be!" runs one passage in the Koran; "they shall dwell in gardens of delight, reposing on silken couches adorned with gold and precious stones, near a flowing river and amidst fruits in abundance. Youths who

will never lose their youthful bloom will go round serving
them with cups and goblets of flowing wine, and their heads
will not ache by drinking nor will it affect their understanding. And there shall accompany them fair damsels having large
black eyes resembling pearls in their shells. Verily, we have
created the damsels of paradise by a peculiar creation; we have
made them virgins, beloved by their husbands, of an equal age
with them, made for their delight."

Sometimes it has been maintained that the Muslim paradise
is for men only, but it is definitely stated in the Koran that
"whoso doeth good works, whether male or female, and is a
true believer, will be admitted into Paradise, and will not in
the least be unjustly dealt with." But it must be admitted that
very little is said of the things that a good woman and wife
may expect to enjoy, and, even in the very early days of his
preaching, Mohammed was suspected of favoring the male
sex in his promises of Heaven.

"Cannot something be done for us women also?" plaintively
demanded one old lady who had been listening to the
Prophet's colorful description; "Will not the Prophet intercede
with Allah that I may be allowed into Paradise?" Whereupon
Mohammed gruffly replied, "No old woman will be admitted
into that glorious abode!" But as his questioner turned away
sorrowing, the warm humanity of the Prophet showed itself.
He called out after her, "Don't worry, Allah will make you
young again!"

Many people, including modern-minded Muslims, have
criticized the Prophet's description of Heaven as being far
too sensuous, and some have argued that its details should not
be taken too literally. However that may be, it should be added
in fairness to Mohammed that he also declared that "those
believers who are in the highest honor with Allah will see the

Divine Face morning and evening, compared with which all other pleasures of Paradise will be lightly esteemed and forgotten."

In the same chapter of the Koran that gives a description of the joys of Heaven, we find an account of the pains of Hell. "How miserable shall the companions of the left hand be! They shall dwell amidst burning winds and scalding water, in the shade of black smoke, that is neither cool nor refreshing. For these are they who enjoyed the pleasures of life when on earth, and said, 'After we have died, and become dust and bones, shall we be raised to life again?' O you men who denied the resurrection, you shall surely eat bitter food and drink boiling water!"

Much more of a similar nature could be quoted, but let us leave this subject and turn to one further item of Muslim belief. This is the doctrine known as predestination, which means that everything that happens, good and evil, has been foreordained by Allah and is in accordance with His will. Muslims are fatalists; they believe that what happens was bound to happen. Every man's fate (we are told) is bound round his neck like a collar. Whether he should be a believer or an unbeliever, obedient to Allah or disobedient, good or bad, and hence be destined to everlasting happiness or eternal misery—it has all been fixed and decided from the very beginning. Nothing he can do can alter it in the slightest.

A harsh doctrine (and one that is also held by many Christians, let it be noted). And yet, side by side with this belief in predestination, in relentless and irrevocable Fate, runs belief in what is called Free Will! A man *can* choose, between good and evil: Allah gives him the power and the opportunity! The two doctrines are absolutely opposed, but the good Muslim professes to believe in both, and finally puts his trust in Allah to do what is right and best.

Tradition has it that when Mohammed lay dying in his room at Medina, his head lying in Ayesha's lap, she put to him this question, O Prophet, does no one enter Paradise except by the mercy of Allah?" "No one," came the answer. "But you, O Prophet," persisted Ayesha, "won't even you enter Paradise except by the compassion of Allah?" Slowly the dying man raised his hand and placed it on his young wife's head. "No," he replied, solemnly, "I shall not enter except Allah cover me with His mercy!"

8

Islam: What a Muslim Does

The religious duties of a Muslim make up what are termed the "Five Pillars of Islam." The first "pillar" is the profession of faith, the *Shahada*, which we have examined in the last chapter; it contains the first words to strike the ear of the newborn Muslim babe and the last to be uttered over the corpse at the grave. The other four "pillars" are the practical requirements of Prayer, Alms-giving, Fasting in the month of Ramadan, and Pilgrimage to Mecca.

Prayer is held to be of such importance that it is called the "Key to Paradise." In the Koran, the Muslim is enjoined to pray three times in the course of the day—at sunset, nightfall, and dawn—but the long-established practice, dating from the Prophet's example, is that prayer should be offered to Allah *five* times daily—at daybreak, noon, mid-afternoon, just after sunset, and when night has fallen.

Wherever he may be, whatever he may be doing, the good Muslim carries out the accustomed ritual of word and posture at the prescribed times, or as near to them as he possibly can. The times are announced by an official of the mosque called the *muezzin* or *mueddin,* from the Arabic for "reciter of the *adhan*" (or prayer).

The first muezzin was the Prophet's Abyssinian slave named Bilal, who was a man with a particularly loud voice; he stood on the flat roof of the Prophet's home at Medina and shouted out the call so that everybody in the city could hear. After a year or two, the Prophet considered using a wooden gong after the fashion of the Christian churches of the time, but ultimately he decided in favor of the human voice. In his time, minarets—the slender towers in the mosques, containing a gallery from which the muezzin makes his call—were unknown, but not long after his death they began to come into general use. The actual wording of the *adhan* has remained as it was ordered by the Prophet; a translation is given on the first page of this book.

Although the ceremonies are not precisely laid down in the Koran, there is no doubt that they, too, are what the Prophet ordered. They are what he used to do himself.

Before he begins to pray, the worshiper must purify himself by ablution, or washing. In the courtyard of every mosque is a tank or basin of clean water, but, if the worshiper is not near a mosque, water from any other source will do as well. If no water is available—when traveling in the desert, for instance—sand may be used instead. The important thing is that the worshiper should do his best to appear before his Maker in as clean a state as possible.

Having tucked up his sleeves a little higher than the elbows,

Before prayer, every Muslim must purify himself by ablution, or washing. Soldiers of the King of Jordan perform their ablutions in a mosque courtyard.

the worshiper washes his hands three times, rinses out his mouth three times by throwing water into it with his right hand, and then does the same with his nostrils. Next, he washes his elbow, taking care to let some water run along his arm from the palm of the hand to the elbow, and then the left hand and arm are washed in the same way. Next, he draws his wetted right hand over the upper part of his head, raising his hat or turban with his left hand. If he has a beard, he combs it with the wetted fingers of his right hand. Now it is the turn for his ears, and then the back of his neck. Finally, he washes his feet as high as the ankles, and passes his fingers between his toes.

For each of these actions there are special words that the worshiper has to recite as he goes through them. In conclusion, he looks down at the ground and says, "I testify that there is no god but Allah, and that Mohammed is the Apostle of Allah."

All this sounds time-consuming, but speed comes with practice, and the whole set of ablutions can be performed in less than a couple of minutes. Nor are they required before each one of the five daily prayers: if the worshiper is quite sure that he has incurred no pollution since the last praying, he may omit them.

On Friday, which is the Muslim day of rest, Muslims are expected to take a complete bath before they say their prayers. It need hardly be said that clean clothes are considered to be as important as clean bodies, and cleanliness is also sought in the ground, mat, carpet, robe, or whatever else it is that the worshiper kneels on. Poor people content themselves with making sure that the ground before them is reasonably clean and dry, but wealthy people have their own prayer carpet, which is about the size of a hearthrug and has a mark on it showing the direction of Mecca.

Each prayer consists of a number of bowings, called *rakahs*, and each rakah consists of seven movements with the appropriate recitations from the Koran.

Standing with his face turned toward Mecca, the worshiper raises his hands on each side of his face and, touching the lobes of his ears with his thumbs, says: *Allahu akbar!* ("God is most great!") Still standing, but with his hands placed before him, a little below his waist he then recites the Fatihah, the opening chapter of the Koran.

Next, the worshiper bows his head and body from the hips, with his hands upon his knees, and says, "I praise the perfection of my Lord, the Great!" Then, straightening up, he repeats, "God is most great!"; after which he drops gently on his knees, places his hands in front of him on the ground, and puts his head between them so that his nose touches the ground. Next he raises himself and sits back on his haunches,

Muslims praying at the Great Mosque in Damascus. Each bow, or *rakah*, consists of seven movements accompanied by the recitation of verses from the Koran.

and then makes a second prostration. With each bowing, he says the words of a prayer. This completes one rakah, and the worshiper rises to his feet and once again declares, *Allahu akbar!*

If the prayer is the one made at daybreak, the worshiper has one more rakah to perform. But if it is the one made at noon, afternoon, or night he must go through four rakahs, while the after-sunset prayer consists of three rakahs.

Although a Muslim may say his prayers anywhere, whenever possible he should say them as a member of the congregation in a mosque under the leadership of a minister called the *imam*. Particularly he should make a point of doing this at noon on Fridays, which day is, as we have just noted, the Muslim Sabbath.

Here it should be noted that an imam is very different from a Christian priest or clergyman: There are no priests in Islam. He is a layman, chosen for his piety and learning to perform the duties of a minister in a part-time capacity, for which he receives a small fee.

The word "mosque" comes to us through the Italian from the Arabic *masjid*, meaning a place of prayer or prostration. The first mosque was erected at Medina under the Prophet's direction, and mosques in all parts of the world have been modeled on it ever since, although there is a vast difference between the splendid mosques of such cities as Baghdad and Cairo and Delhi and the little building of earth and tree trunks that Mohammed designed.

Every mosque must have a courtyard and one or more fountains for ablutions. This area is often very spacious, and in hot countries it may be used for worship. Within the court is a building which in general pattern is similar to a church. The *mihrab*, a semicircular recess or niche in the wall, facing the entrance, takes the place of the altar or communion table; this marks the direction of Mecca, toward which worshipers must turn when performing their devotions. To the right is a pulpit, usually of plain wood, and facing it is a lectern on which lies a copy of the Koran. There are no seats. The walls are usually perfectly bare, beyond perhaps a few verses from the Koran. There are no stained-glass windows; there are no memorial tablets, and no statues or holy pictures—because the Prophet sternly forbade them.

The first thing a Muslim does on entering the precincts is to take off his shoes, which he then carries in his left hand, sole to sole. Then he makes his way to the fountain or tank, and performs his ablutions, after which he takes his place in a row with other worshipers, facing the mihrab, and goes through the ritual of prayer outlined above. He places his slippers or shoes on the ground in front of him.

In Mohammed's time it seems that, at first, women joined the men in the public prayers in the mosque, but he did not favor the practice and it was dropped. In some mosques, however, there are special places at the back of the building for women. The worshipers are usually very plainly but neatly dressed; it is against Muslim ideas of what is right and proper to come into God's House in rich apparel, and wealthy people lay aside their ornaments when they enter the mosque, for fear of being suspected of showing off in the presence of Allah and their fellow worshipers.

There is no music, no choir, no congregational singing, but the words of the prayers are solemnly intoned. The proceedings are strikingly impressive, as the ranks of worshipers at a given signal hold themselves erect, prostrate themselves with their foreheads touching the ground, then at another signal rise as one man, all the time reciting the words laid down from the time of the Prophet. Sometimes after prayers there will be a sermon, delivered by the imam, and this will consist usually of the reading and exposition of a passage from the Koran. But Muslim worship is mainly prayer and praise.

Many years ago, an English traveler named E. W. Lane paid tribute to the behavior of Muslims in their mosques. "The

utmost solemnity and decorum are observed in the public
worship of the Muslims," he wrote in his very readable book,
Manners and Customs of the Modern Egyptians. "Their looks
and behavior in the mosque are not those of enthusiastic devotion but of calm and modest piety. Never are they guilty
of a designedly irregular word or action during their prayers.
They appear wholly absorbed in the adoration of their
Creator; humble and downcast, yet without affected humility,
or a forced expression of countenance."

A much more recent tribute is paid by Professor Alfred
Guillaume, in his book *Islam.* "A Christian who, like the
writer," he says "goes from a visit to the Church of the Holy
Sepulchre with its warring, noisy, competitive sects to the
peace and devotion of the Great Mosque in Jerusalem cannot
but be saddened and chastened to find in the one what he was
looking for in the other." Many other writers have said very
much the same. They have found that the mosque is indeed a
house of prayer.

Next to prayer comes alms-giving. Beggars are very plenti-
ful in Oriental countries, where Islam is most usual, and the
good Muslim should never allow to go unheeded the voice
that begs him for alms "in the name of Allah" or "for the love
of Allah." In earlier days there was, in addition to this volun-
tary alms-giving, a poor tax called *zakat,* or "Allah's share,"
which was put at one-fortieth of a man's income and was
collected by civil servants. Today, the amount is left to the
conscience of the individual, but it is the accepted thing for
Muslims to give something to the poor and needy at weddings
and funerals and other important occasions. Such gifts were
encouraged, even ordered, by the Prophet. "If you are
charitable in public," says the Koran, "good, but it is better
still to give alms to the poor in secret, and it will atone for

your sins; God knows well enough what you do." And Mohammed is said to have declared that a man who does not give alms will have a serpent twisted round his neck at the resurrection.

The third of the practical requirements, or acts of devotion, is fasting. Here again the influence of the Prophet is most marked. "You can't please God without fasting," he is reported to have said, and he also declared that fasting is the "Gate of Religion."

"O true believers," runs the passage in the Koran that enjoins the practice, "a fast is ordained you that you may fear God. You shall fast a certain number of days, but those among you who are sick or on a journey shall fast an equal number of other days. And those who can keep it, and don't, must redeem their neglect by maintaining a poor man [for a year]. But if you *do* fast, it will be the better for you, if you but knew it."

The fast continues for thirty days, throughout Ramadan, the month in which the Koran was first revealed to Mohammed. Exceptionally devout Muslims may, however, extend the fast to forty days, in imitation of what is believed to have been the practice of the Prophet and his family. From sunrise, or the time when "you can plainly distinguish a white thread from a black thread by the daybreak," until sunset, nothing whatever is allowed to pass the lips in the way of food and drink. No tobacco must be smoked, no perfume inhaled, no bath taken. A man should strive even to avoid swallowing his saliva.

The obligations of Ramadan are as binding on women as on men, but small children are exempt, as are mothers with babies, and old people, as well as those who are sick or are traveling, as mentioned in the passage from the Koran just quoted. But whenever possible, those excused are expected to make up for the omission by fasting at a later date.

Since the Muslim calendar is a lunar one (based on the moon), unlike our solar calendar (based on the sun), the months may over a period of years fall in different seasons. Lent, the period of religious fasting observed among Christians, always falls in the spring, but Ramadan may fall sometimes in summer and sometimes in winter. When it falls in summer, the fast may be extraordinarily severe. For the rich man in his comfortable home it requires great discipline not to be allowed to take even a sip of water when the temperature is over 100° F. in the shade; but for the poor laborer toiling in the hot sun it must be a dreadful ordeal. Yet, the fast is most generally observed, and many Muslims would sooner give up their prayers than evade the obligations of Ramadan.

At dusk, when you can no longer distinguish between the two threads, the fast is broken for the night. Believers may then take what refreshment they like, but since a full meal after twelve or fourteen hours of complete abstinence might be dangerous, "breaking the fast" is done by stages. First a cooling drink is taken, or a few sips of boiling water, or a little spinach strained through muslin. Some people prefer a cup of tea, and some say that there is nothing to equal a good pinch of salt. Then may come dried fruits, dates, figs, sugared almonds, etc., which have been placed ready on a tray; glasses of sherbet made of sugar and water are handed round, pipes are brought out, cigarettes lit. After this, it is time for evening prayers, and then the family will sit down to a good square meal, followed perhaps by music and dancing. But, with daybreak, the fast starts again.

So it goes throughout the month of Ramadan, and then, when it has come to its end, there is a festival—one of the most important and joyful in the Muslim year. Everybody puts on new clothes and goes to morning prayers in the mosque. Presents are given to relations and friends and servants. Visits are paid, and women in particular go to the cemeteries and place palm branches on the graves of their loved ones.

Now we come to the duty of pilgrimage to the Kaaba at Mecca. Tradition says that Mohammed once declared that a Muslim who died without having visited the Holy House at Mecca might just as well have died a Jew or a Christian. But there is reason to believe that when he was living in Medina he would have liked to abolish the pilgrimage to Mecca, since it was so closely associated with Arab paganism. The time-honored practice was too strong for him, however, and he had to content himself with the abolition of its idolatrous accompaniments. The idols were destroyed, but the Holy House was preserved and constituted the holiest shrine of Islam. This masterly stroke of statesmanship secured him the support of the Meccans. By word of mouth and by personal example, he showed that the pilgrimage to Mecca was now a recognized and essential part of the faith of Islam. In the Koran we are told that "it is the duty of all those who are able to go and visit the Kaaba at Mecca."

The pilgrimage is called the *hajj,* and every Muslim ought to become at least once in his lifetime a *hajji.* The duty is laid on women as well as on men, but the great majority of the pilgrims have always been men, for the good reason that women in Arabia and other Eastern lands shrink from being seen in public. The procedure is that prescribed by tradition, and in the main it is what was observed centuries before the coming of Islam.

One change introduced by the Prophet was in the matter of

costume. The original ritual required that the pilgrims should be nude, but Mohammed ordered that when they came within the sacred territory of Mecca they should lay aside their clothes and don a special garment called the *ihram*. For men, this consists of two pieces of cotton cloth about the size of bath towels, one of which is fastened round the waist and the other is thrown over the shoulders. The head should be completely shaved, but beards are left on. The nails must be carefully trimmed. The feet must be covered with a special kind of slipper or sandal, which "covers neither the heel nor the instep."

Female pilgrims wear a less revealing costume, comprising five garments—trousers, overdress, green frock, black robe, and veil.

During the pilgrimage, the pilgrim must not shave, cut his nails, oil his head, or even scratch his skin. He must not hunt or catch birds (but he may fish), and this precept is so faithfully followed that he will not kill even a louse or a flea. It is permissible, however, to kill certain noxious animals such as kites and scorpions—and dogs that bite. All quarreling must be avoided. A constant watch must be kept on every word and action. Men are advised to keep women at a distance, for fear of being distracted from the holy business that has brought them to the place.

Having arrived in the city itself, the first thing to be done is to walk round the Kaaba seven times, beginning at the southeast corner in which the famous Stone is embedded in the wall, 4 or 5 feet above the ground. The Stone is described as an irregular oval, about 7 inches in diameter, and broken into a dozen pieces that have been stuck together again. Its color is now a deep reddish brown, and it is contained in a silver band. The Kaaba itself is about 40 feet by 35 feet and

50 feet in height, built of layers of gray stone, and generally covered with a black curtain. There is a door about 7 feet from the ground, but the walls are windowless. Inside there are three wooden pillars supporting the roof, and there is no furnishing other than a number of gold and silver lamps.

For the first three circuits, the pilgrims use a short, quick step, and then, for the rest, one that is slow and dignified. This procedure was ordered, it seems, by the Prophet. At each turn, the Stone is reverently kissed or touched as a tribute not of worship but of reverence.

The next ceremony is partly to run and partly to walk seven times between two little mounds, called Safa, and Marwa, a short distance away; this is because, according to ancient tradition, Hagar ran back and forth seven times between these two little hills looking for a spring of water for her son Ishmael, who was dying of thirst, following which the well Zem-zem made its miraculous appearance in the desert. Next, the pilgrims visit another mount called Arafat, twelve miles from Mecca; here they spend the day, and the following night is spent nearby in prayer and reading the Koran. In the morning, they visit some other sacred monuments, and then hurry away to the valley of Mina, in which are three pillars. At each of these, the pilgrim must throw seven stones. This is called "stoning the Devil," and it is said to be in imitation of "Father Abraham," who was once disturbed in his devotions on this spot by the Devil and drove him off with stones. On the tenth day of the pilgrimage, sacrifices are offered to Allah, using a camel, a sheep, or other horned domestic animals. Some of the meat is eaten by the pilgrims, and the rest is given to the poor.

Tradition decrees that the best month for the pilgrimage is the twelfth of the Muslim year, but there is a constant stream

Pilgrims circling the Kaaba at the Great Mosque in Mecca. The heavy covering, which glorifies and protects the shrine, has been pulled back to disclose the door.

of pilgrims on their way from distant parts of Asia and Central Africa. To begin with, just two or three men set out from their village, and their numbers are added to as they go along, until they constitute a caravan. Then caravan is added to caravan, until there is a mighty host making for the holy city.

The largest groups come from southern Arabia—Yemen in particular—and from Iraq, Syria, and Egypt. Some are on foot, others on camelback. They trade, they beg, they work their way. Some die by the wayside and are then regarded as martyrs. At long last, the survivors strike a Red Sea port, whence they are carried across in Arab dhows (single-masted sailing ships), or they come down the coast in ships from Suez. Altogether the number of pilgrims may reach 250,000 in a year.

The importance of the pilgrimage can hardly be over-estimated. Men of different races—Negroes, Persians, Syrians, Egyptians, Turks, Pakistanis, Arabs, Chinese—rich and poor, old and young, mix on terms of absolute equality. They dress alike; they eat alike; they perform the same acts of worship. On their way to Mecca, they see quite a lot of the world, and their eyes are opened to new and different ways of living. Since trading is allowed, a good craftsman may find a better place to settle than his home town. The pilgrims compare notes, and sometimes their rulers wish they didn't. But the really important thing is that they realize as probably never before that Islam is a great, world-wide brotherhood, in which each one of them has a place. Race doesn't matter; color doesn't matter; social class doesn't matter: Only right belief matters.

The great majority of the pilgrims go no farther than Mecca, but those who can afford the time and expense proceed to Medina, the burial place of the Prophet. The Masjid al-Nabi (Mosque of the Prophet) is second in importance only to the Kaaba at Mecca. In one corner is the Hujra, or "chamber," which was originally the hut that Ayesha shared with the Prophet. When he died, he was laid to rest beneath its floor, and there he is believed to lie, his body undecayed, on his right side with his face turned toward Mecca. The interior of the mausoleum is hung with costly curtains—behind which are the tombs of Mohammed, Abu Bakr, and Umar—and, a slight distance apart, so as not to offend Muslim ideas of decorum and the lady's own sense of decency, is the tomb of the Lady Fatima, the Prophet's favorite daughter and the wife of his cousin and devoted disciple Ali. Beyond Umar's tomb is the space left vacant for Isa, as the Muslims call Jesus.

Pilgrims are not allowed to enter the Hujra, but they may peer into its interior through some small windows. Very often they are overcome with emotion at finding themselves in the place hallowed by memories of the Prophet's life and death, and the more impressionable among them even claim that, above the tomb, visible from a distance, is a kind of celestial light.

The pilgrimage completed, the pilgrims may now attend to their appearance and change to their ordinary clothes. There follows a period of relaxation and of indulgence in the pleasures that the town affords. Then they take the homeward road. Already, perhaps, the pilgrim is wearing a green turban, which is an indication of the fact that he has been to Mecca.

So much for the four "Pillars" of practical devotion. Sometimes mention is made of another—the *jihad*, or holy war against the enemies of Allah. In the Koran, this is stated more than once to be a sacred duty, but it is clear that Mohammed did not intend that his followers should be in a state of constant war with non-Muslims. On the contrary, he showed himself extraordinarily tolerant of other faiths. He expressly ordered that the Muslims should not be the aggressors, and laid it down that "people of the Book"—Jews and Christians —were to be allowed to enjoy their lives and property under

Muslim rule, as long as they obeyed the laws and paid a special tax.

From time to time, rulers of the world of Islam have proclaimed *jihad* against non-Muslims, for instance, in 1914, when the Sultan of Turkey tried to enlist the whole Muslim world against Britain and France on the side of the Germans in World War I.

Now for some things the Muslim must *not* do. The Koran expressly forbids intoxicating liquors. This prohibition is due to the Prophet, who is said to have been scandalized when he learned that one of his neighbors had tried to say family prayers when drunk. Whereupon the Prophet had a fresh passage added to the Koran: "O true believers, do not come to prayers when you are drunk." Another passage runs, "Wine is an abomination of the work of Satan; therefore avoid it, if you would prosper." But it must be admitted that the Prophet's ban very often goes unheeded.

More successful has been his prohibition of pork. Muslims, indeed, have an absolute horror of eating pig meat, and regard with loathing people who dine off such "unclean" food. One of the causes of the great Indian Mutiny of 1857 was the suspicion on the part of the Muslim soldiers that the new cartridges that had been issued to them by the British rulers had been greased with pig's fat, and many a bloody riot has broken out in India when Hindus have been suspected of smearing pig blood on the walls of mosques.

Several reasons have been given for the Prophet's ban, and none are altogether satisfactory. It has been said that one can develop the disease trichinosis through eating pork—but the early Muslims knew very little about trichinosis. It has been said that pork is too rich for a hot climate—but many days in Arabia and the Orient are cold enough, and roast pork probably tastes the same in Mecca as it does in London or New York. Another and more ingenious reason put forward is that pigs eat acorns and beech nuts and the like, and, since there are not enough of these in Arabia, food has to be specially imported for the pigs, or they must be fed on food that people might eat. Perhaps wine was banned originally for a similar reason; grapes don't grow in the Hijaz—wine must be imported and paid for with money that might be better spent on local produce.

Gambling is sternly forbidden in the Koran, together with the casting of lots and "arrows," which seems to have been a kind of divination or attempt at telling the future. Some Muslim commentators have argued that Mohammed meant by "lots" all games of chance, including cards and dice. Chess is usually allowed, since it depends entirely on skill, but, even so, it must not be played for money, and there must be no betting on the result by the spectators. Occasionally, it has been urged that the good Muslim should refrain from taking coffee—and this in the land that is the home of the coffee plant. Smoking is allowed by all except the most severe moralists, and another questionable practice is the taking of opium.

Although there is nothing in the Koran exactly comparable to the Ten Commandments of the Old Testament, most of the ten are mentioned separately. Idolatry and the making of images, murder, sabbath-breaking, adultery, theft, bearing false witness, covetousness, neglect of parents—the things that Moses declared to be absolutely condemned by Jehovah were just as strongly denounced by Mohammed in the name of Allah.

One special crime should be added to the list. In Mohammed's day, as from time immemorial, it was the custom among the pagan Arabs to get rid of unwanted girl babies by taking them out into the desert, burying them up to the neck in the sand, and leaving them to their fate. This practice horrified Mohammed, and he moved heaven and earth to suppress it. "Don't kill your children for fear of being brought to want," he urged in more than one passage in the Koran; "the slaying of them is a great sin. The Lord will provide for them, and for you." So strongly did he feel about the matter that, in the list of great, earth-shaking events that he prophesied would herald the Last Day, he included a reference to it. "The infant girl who has been buried alive shall be asked for what crime she was put to death." "At that time," he warned solemnly, "each soul shall know what it has done."

For children, the Prophet always had a kindly word, and he was also most considerate in his treatment of the old. "Show kindness to your parents," he urged his followers; "if they grow old under your roof, don't be impatient with them or grumble at them, but speak to them kindly. Treat then gently and with respect, and say, 'Lord, be merciful unto them; they nursed me when I was little.' "

From first to last, Mohammed was concerned with the way of life that is acceptable to Allah. He felt it was his mission to make "true believers" in word and deed. Perhaps the best summary of his ideal is given in the second chapter of the Koran: "The good man believes in Allah and the Last Day, and the angels, and the scriptures, and the prophets. For Allah's sake he looks after his relations, and orphans, and those in want, the stranger and the beggar. He redeems the captive. He is constant in prayers, gives alms, keeps his promises, bears himself patiently in adversity and time of war. The people who do these things are the true believers: they are the people who really love Allah."

9

Mohammed the Prophet of Islam

Mohammed has been dead more than 1,300 years, but his influence is probably greater today than ever before. Certainly it affects more people, for some 400 million of the world's present population belong to Islam.

The story of its expansion is a fascinating one, but we have no room to tell it here. In these final pages, we must get back to the Prophet himself and think of the way in which he has proved a pathfinder to untold millions of men. His personal example has been, and still is, of tremendous importance.

No sooner was he dead than his sorrowing disciples began to collect his sayings and the reports of things that he had done or permitted to be done. Before very long, a vast mass of *hadiths*, or statements made by or about Mohammed, had accumulated, and the time came when it had to be examined and sorted out and put in order. The man mainly responsible for this work was a Muslim scholar named al-Bukhari, who died about A.D. 870; he wrote a book on the subject that contains 3,450 chapters and in which about 7,300 hadiths are quoted as being authoritative. Later Muslim tradition asserted that Bukhari made this selection out of some 200,000 hadiths— proof surely of the enormous importance attached to the Prophet's memory. To this day, the life of the individual Muslim man and woman is largely guided, first, by the Koran but, then, almost as powerfully, by the *Sunna*, or traditional teaching of the Prophet. On these two, the Koran and the Sunna, is built the magnificent body of Islamic law, which has been well described as the master science of the Muslim world.

Mohammed, as we have noted more than once, was an unlettered man; he may never have been able to read a book. But he had the highest respect for knowledge. "The ink of the scholar is more holy than the blood of the martyrs," runs one hadith; and another, "He who leaves home in search of knowledge walks in the path of Allah." A third is more explicit: "Knowledge is our friend in the desert, our society in solitude, our companion when bereft of friends; it guides us to happiness, it sustains us in misery, it serves as an armor against enemies."

In the light of such encouragement, Muslims devoted themselves to study and teaching with marked success. As a people, the Arabs were largely unlettered, but they received the gift of learning from their subjects, and, throughout the Middle Ages, the Muslim universities and schools were far ahead of those in Christendom. Muslims were generally more tolerant of scientific learning than the Christians were, and astronomy and other sciences were able to make progress among them unhampered by theological opposition. Mohammed is supposed to have declared that there are two main sciences—the science of God, which is theology, and the science of Man, which is medicine. Muslim doctors became famed throughout the West, and Muslim ideas of sanitation were equally advanced. Cordova, which was the chief town of the Moorish, or Muslim, kingdom in Spain for nearly three centuries, is reported to have possessed 700 mosques and 900 public baths. The story of the Muslims in Spain is, indeed, one of the most romantic in the history of Europe, but there is no space to tell it here.

The outstanding contribution of Islam to literature is, of course, the Koran, which was given to the world through Mohammed. He wrote nothing himself—at least, so far as we know—but he inspired others to write, and his life provided biographers for centuries with a theme that they delighted to develop. In art, his influence has been more direct. He was strongly opposed to idolatry, and he condemned outright the making of images; at the Day of Judgment (he is reported to have said), the maker of images or pictures of anybody or anything with life will have his works placed in front of him and will be ordered to put life into them; as he won't be able to do this, he will for his presumption be cast forthwith into Hell. Fortunately, the prohibition is taken as referring only to people and animals; vegetable life does not come under the ban, and so in mosques the decoration is mainly floral, supplemented by ornamental writing to which the flowing Arabic script is admirably suited. Muslim ornamentation is primarily what is called "arabesque."

Incidentally, it is because of this prohibition that one never finds pictures of the Prophet in Muslim books. To Muslims, such would appear to be blasphemous.

Mohammed did not like music, very likely because it had

been so intimately associated with pagan rites. Moreover, in his time, it had a decidedly immoral flavor; the musicians, singers, and performers on tambourines and flutes, reed pipes, or oboes were usually slaves of both sexes imported from Syria and Persia and of a notoriously loose manner of living. In one of his hadiths, the Prophet is reported to have said that a musical instrument is the muezzin of the Devil. But, in this instance at least, Mohammed has been unable to carry his people with him. The love of music was so deep and widespread among the Muslim peoples that they dared to disobey their Prophet's injunction, and music became one of the arts in which everybody delighted and many excelled. But there is still no music in the mosque or the ritual of religion wherever it may be practiced.

In architecture, Mohammed favored the extremely simple, but this may have been because his resources were so slight. The first mosque was the one he had built at Medina, and it was plain in the extreme. Before long, however, the mosques became splendid buildings as befitted the worship of Allah, and among them are some of the most lovely buildings in the world.

Those features that are typical of "Saracenic" architecture —the great domes and slender minarets, the pointed arches, and the arabesque ornamentation—owe nothing to the Prophet. They are due to the special circumstances of the countries in which they arose, of which the imaginative genius of the architects was not the least.

Few of the sciences had made their appearance in Mohammed's time. It can be said that the Prophet's insistence on the kiblah made it essential for Muslim builders to study geography, since they had to know with accuracy the direction of Mecca. Mohammed, as a young man wandering at night in

the desert, had studied the stars, and this may well have encouraged his disciples to practice astronomy. Certainly, in this
field of study, the Muslims were long supreme, and they were
not hampered by any preconceived notions about the uni-
verse, such as those that had delayed astronomical studies in
Christian Europe. The study of geography was also furthered
by the development of the pilgrim traffic to Mecca from all
parts, and by the ease and security with which travelers might
pass from one end to another of the immense empire of the
Caliphs, or "Successors," of Mohammed.

Another thing that Mohammed encouraged was so basic
and simple that it is hardly ever mentioned: hard work. He
taught that labor is a duty, not something that should be
pushed off at every opportunity onto the shoulders of the
poor and slaves. As we have seen, he did his own housework,
and we may be sure that he dug his own garden and vegetable
plot. He recommended commerce and agriculture as things
that are meritorious in the sight of God, with the result that
Muslim traders and farmers became highly efficient.

Muslim historians have tried to show that culture under
Islam has not been confined to men, and many instances could
be cited of Muslim ladies who have won success in literature
and have devoted themselves to scientific activities. But there
is no denying that the Prophet looked upon women as not
only the weaker but also the inferior sex. "Men have authority
over women," runs a text in the Koran, "because God has
made the one superior to the other and because men spend
their wealth to maintain them." This is a hard saying in the
ears of those devoted women who in Morocco and Egypt and
other Muslim countries have been striving, not without success, to raise the deplorably low status of their sex.

As already pointed out, Mohammed did not invent polyg-

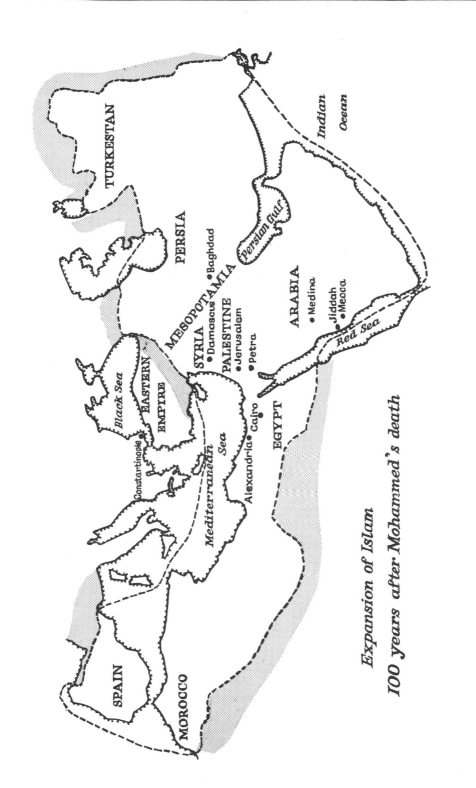

Expansion of Islam
100 years after Mohammed's death

amy, and he certainly did much to improve the condition of women in the polygamous society in which he found himself, just as he improved the lot of orphans and children and slaves. But, by his personal example, he threw the mantle of respectability over polygamy, even though he did not insist that a Muslim male *must* have four wives. In the enlightened Muslim lands today, attempts are being made to modify the Prophet's teaching and practical example in this respect, and the demand is being increasingly made that the rule should be one husband to one wife.

Mohammed's rather poor opinion of women is also shown by his statement that, while there have been many perfect men, there have been only *four* perfect women! The first was a woman named Asiyah who, according to Mohammed, was the wife of the Pharaoh under whom the Children of Israel left Egypt; she is unknown in history. The second was Mary, the mother of Jesus. The third was Khadija, Mohammed's first wife. And the fourth was Fatima, his favorite daughter, who married Ali; she is described as being of altogether estimable character. These four ladies were put before the women of Islam as examples of what good women should be, and, ever since, Muslim women have tried to follow in the footsteps of these perfect ones and so receive the favor of Allah and His Prophet.

But it is not through art, literature, science, or law that the Prophet has exercised his greatest influence, but rather as the preacher of a new religion. For hundreds of years, Islam was propagated by the sword, and its conquests were as easy as they were sweeping; in lands that for centuries had been nominally Christian, the common people gladly welcomed the soldiers of the Prophet and hastened to adopt the religion of Allah. But, after a while, the storm of war died down, and

Islam was carried far and wide by missionaries trudging across the deserts of Central Asia or through the jungles of Africa, preaching the faith of the Prophet.

There is something in Islam that makes a strong appeal to the lowly and humble of mankind. Its message is clear; its requirements are easily understood, if not always easy to perform. In Islam, there is no color bar—all men are brothers under Allah. And, to the simple peasant, the figure of the Prophet Mohammed has a comforting assurance. He was a good man, but was not too good to be true; he was a humble man who rose to greatness yet never forgot the humbleness of his origins; he was a kindly man who felt pity for the poor and downtrodden and dispossessed, the widow and the orphan, the children and the aged. But Muslim missionaries also meet with opposition and indifference. The cornerstone of Islam is its belief in God, and in many countries today the prevailing mood is secular. To many young men in the coffee shops and bazaars of Cairo and Lagos, Tashkent, Karachi and Baghdad, the Prophet seems old-fashioned, and his example is blamed for holding back many social and political reforms.

So, after thirteen centuries, Mohammed is still a storm center, as he was in the days when he first set himself against the chiefs of the Koreish in his native city. But the faith he proclaimed has become one of the world's great religions. Today, in thousands of minarets in scores of countries stretching across the globe from North Africa to China, the muezzins are mounting the stairs, and soon, standing where all may see and hear them, they will proclaim the call that first came from Mohammed's lips:

Allahu akbar! God is most great!
. . . Mohammed is God's Apostle!

Table of Dates

Suggestions for Further Reading

ALI, A. YUSUF. *The Message of Islam*. New York: Paragon Book Reprint, 1956.

ANDERSON, J. N. D. *Islamic Law in the Modern World*. New York: New York University Press, 1961.

ANDERSON, J. N. D. (ed.). *Family Law in Asia and Africa*. New York: Frederick A. Praeger, 1968.

ARBERRY, A. J. *The Koran Interpreted*. New York: Macmillan, 1964.

AZZAM, ABDUL RAHMAN. *Eternal Message of Mohammad*. New York: Devin-Adair, 1964; paperback ed., New York: New American Library, 1965.

CRAGG, KENNETH. *Call of the Minaret*. New York: Oxford University Press, 1957.

GIBB, HAMILTON A. R. *Mohammedanism: An Historical Survey*, 2d ed., rev.; New York: Oxford University Press, 1961; paperback ed., 1962.

GIBB, HAMILTON A. R. *Studies on the Civilization of Islam*, ed. WILLIAM R. POLK and STANFORD J. SHAW. Boston: Beacon Press, 1962.

KRITZECK, JAMES (ed.). *Anthology of Islamic Literature*. New York: Holt, Rinehart & Winston, 1964; paperback ed., New York: New American Library, 1966.

LEVY, REUBEN. *Social Structure of Islam*. New York: Cambridge University Press, 1957.

LICHTENSTADTER, ILSE. *Islam and the Modern Age*. New York: Twayne, 1959.

LINCOLN, CHARLES E. *Black Muslims in America*. Boston: Beacon Press, 1962.

MORGAN, KENNETH W. *Islam: The Straight Path*. New York: Ronald Press, 1958.

NUTTING, ANTHONY. *The Arabs*. New York: Clarkson N. Potter, 1963; paperback ed., New York: New American Library, 1965.

SMITH, WILFRED CANTWELL. *Islam in Modern History*. Princeton, N.J.: Princeton University Press, 1957; paperback ed., New York: New American Library, 1959.

The Koran. Translated by N. J. DAWOOD. Baltimore: Penguin, 1956.

The Meaning of the Glorious Koran: An Explanatory Translation. Translated by MOHAMMED MARMADUKE PICKTHALL. New York: New American Library, 1954.

TRIMINGHAM, J. SPENCER. *The Influence of Islam upon Africa*. New York: Frederick A. Praeger, 1968.

WATT, W. MONTGOMERY. *Muhammad, Prophet and Statesman*. New York: Oxford University Press, 1961.

WOODSMALL, RUTH F. *Women and the New East*. Washington, D.C.: Middle East Institute, 1962.

Index